YOU CAN GET PAST YOUR PAST BY ACCEPTING GOD'S LOVE

Lorna Foster Richards

You Can Get Past Your Past by Accepting God's Love

Copyright © 2025 by Lorna Foster Richards

ISBN: 978-1-969978-29-6

DEDICATION

The Holy Spirit who has been my inspiration.

This book is dedicated to everyone who has been looked down upon, ashamed, bitter, hurt, and has been constantly reminded of their past life, or is even going through it now.

Dedicated to my darling husband, who stood by me for over 18 years, encouraged me, loved me, and makes me feel special knowing that my past doesn't define me.

Dedicated to my family. They are so special and stood by me through my life. They never looked down on me. Sisters, brother, children, nieces, nephews, and other relatives. They have encouraged me to continue writing.

ACKNOWLEDGEMENTS

I want to acknowledge some wonderful people who prayed me up and encouraged me, reminding me that I can make it.

Sis. Carlene Leachman

Sis. Joyce Reid

Sis. Coral Chambers

Sis. Sophia Wilson

Sis. Dennes Thompson

Sis. Naomi Thompson

To the entire West Bay congregation, under the leadership of Bishop Clovis Wilks, Rev. Wilks, and the other ministers. Thank you for constantly praying for me. God bless you.

I have been writing this book for over 20 years, and it seemed like I could never finish it. But God opened the way, and I am truly grateful. I knew the Holy Spirit was speaking to me, but I was ashamed to let anyone know what I had been through. Now I understand that my past is my past.

I want to use this story to encourage someone.

I would also like to extend my heartfelt thanks to **Opeyemi Adebanjo** for their invaluable support and contributions.

TABLE OF CONTENT

INTRODUCTION

Everyone has a past, and although some may try to bury it under silence, numb it with distractions, or deny its grip by pretending it never happened, the truth is that the past has a way of speaking into the present and even threatening the future when you are not careful. I know this not because I read it somewhere or heard someone else's story, but because I lived it. My past was so rough, so devastating, and so painfully real that it nearly destroyed me. I carried wounds so deep that they left me convinced I would never truly heal, and I bore chains so heavy that I was certain I would never be free. There were nights when I thought it was all over, nights when hope seemed like a distant stranger, and mornings when rising from bed felt like an impossible task.

Perhaps, as you read these words, you know exactly what I mean because you too are carrying something heavy, something you would rather not talk about, something you wish you could erase from your history. Maybe it was abuse, betrayal, rejection, failure, or mistakes you made that you can't stop replaying in your mind. Maybe it was a heartbreak that shattered you so completely that you still feel the broken pieces cutting inside your soul. Or maybe it was something so private that nobody else even knows about it, yet it has stolen your joy, your laughter, and the very fire that once made life worth living. Believe me, I understand because I have been there, and I can tell you with certainty that the pain is real, the scars are real, but so is the healing power of God's love when you accept it.

The Spirit of God led me to write this book not because I needed something else to do with my time, but because He had you in mind. That is right, you. You may feel unseen or forgotten, but I assure you that heaven knows your name, and God has been watching over your life even in the moments when you thought He had abandoned you. The reality is that your past does not define you, and while it may have robbed you of years, of joy, of peace, and even of your sense of self, it does not have the final say. The One who created you, the One who formed you with intention and breathed life into you, is more than able to step into your story and rewrite what the enemy tried to destroy.

When I look back at my own life, I see a trail of brokenness that could have been the end of me. I see decisions that I regret, mistakes that almost cost me everything, and pains that made me question whether life was even worth living. However, in the middle of that darkness, God's light found me, and His love rescued me. In the midst of that storm, His hand reached for me, and what I discovered is that the love of God cannot be hindered by your past, it is not intimidated by your scars, and it is never deterred by your failures. His love is greater, stronger, and deeper than anything you have ever faced, and that love is what brought this book to you.

I want you to know from the very beginning that this is not just another book filled with nice words, principles, or motivational sayings. This is a divine appointment, a sacred conversation, and a lifeline extended from God's heart to yours. The pages you are about to read are more than ink and paper; they are vessels of grace, healing, and restoration. They are the Spirit's way of saying, "You are not forgotten, you are not too far gone, and you are not beyond redemption."

You may feel unworthy, but let me remind you that God specializes in using broken vessels, scarred lives, and shattered pieces. You may feel disqualified, but rest assured, His grace qualifies you. You may feel like the past has robbed you of too much time, but trust me on this:

God is able to redeem the years that the enemy stole. And while you may not be able to go back and change the beginning of your story, I want you to know that you can, with His help, start today and change the ending.

As you read these chapters, I want you to open your heart to the possibility that change is not only possible, but inevitable when you allow God's love into the deepest places of your life. I want you to see that the chains that have bound you can truly be broken, the lies that have haunted you can be silenced, and the joy that has been stolen can be restored.

So, as you begin this journey with me, I invite you to lean in, to read not just with your eyes but with your spirit, and to let every word remind you that you are loved, you are chosen, and you are called. This is more than my story; this is your story too, because the same God who lifted me is ready to lift you, the same God who healed me is ready to heal you, and the same God who gave me a new beginning is waiting to give you one as well.

CHAPTER ONE

THE STORY OF MY LIFE

The Child Who Laughed but Changed Along the Way

When I think back to my childhood, one thing that always stands out is that I usually laughed a lot. My laughter was free, it was innocent, and it came so easily, probably because life felt simple then. I laughed without wondering who was watching or what they thought about me, and I laughed because it was natural. But as I grew into my teenage years, that laughter slowly faded away. I still don't know how it happened. I did not plan for it to disappear, and I did not know what had changed, but I just suddenly realized I was no longer the girl who laughed freely. You see, this is one of the strange parts of growing up. As a child, you usually live in a world where everything feels light, but when you step into your teenage years, you start asking questions you cannot always answer and may not even get answers to from other people. That was how it happened for me. I tried to make sense of myself, but the truth is, I could not. I went to school, I tried hard to make friends, but I never felt like I could communicate with people the way others did. I watched others laugh and talk freely, and I wondered why I was different.

There was a longing inside me that I could not put into words. I wanted to be loved, and I wanted someone to see me and care for me. I wanted to feel like I mattered to someone outside of my family. Don't get me wrong, my family cared for me, and I knew they loved me in their own way, but it seemed as if nobody could truly understand what I was going through inside. I was reaching out for something I could not even name, but the harder I tried, the emptier I seemed to feel. Maybe you can relate to that, right? Maybe you have felt the same hunger for love and acceptance. I am talking about that restless sense that something is missing, and no one around you seems to notice how deeply you are struggling. It is a painful place to be in because while others are living their lives, you may be silently asking yourself, 'Why do I feel this way? What is wrong with me?' These are some of the very questions that seem to linger in the mind of millions of people, and I can say it is some of these very kinds of questions that followed me into the decisions I made later, decisions that shaped my life in ways I did not fully see at the time.

Early Motherhood and the Struggle for Love

Painfully speaking, at the age of fifteen I got pregnant, and because of that, I had to drop out of school. That loss was really deep because I had been trying so hard to make it in school. Even after I left, I kept feeling very bad about myself because just as I was beginning to make some friends, I had to leave them and watch my life begin to crash. This made me feel even lonelier and convinced me that time and life were against me. I thought I had been building something when I was at school, but now, suddenly, it had disappeared. Something else is that the real hurt was not simply the ending of classes but the breaking of hope and the sudden sense that the future I had imagined was now gone.

Getting pregnant for this man, I thought there was something special and good about him, and I thought I loved him, but the truth is I didn't know what real love was because what I was really doing was trying to fill the empty space inside me that had been growing since my laughter left. I believed that having him, holding him, or securing his attention would make the hollow inside me smaller, and so when pregnancy came, I thought I had finally found a way to make my life matter, but I only discovered that an empty heart cannot be filled by another human being. You must hear this clearly and always remember it: "Trying to make someone love you the way a man should love a woman will never heal your deepest emptiness because you are carrying wounds that are not theirs to fix."

My family cared for me, and they tried to help because they loved me, and I will always be grateful for that support, yet there was a loneliness that practical help could not reach because what I needed was someone to touch the inside of my life and speak truth there. But then again, at that age I did not know how to ask or where to find such a touch. I cried many days and nights, needing someone to tell me I was special and worthy, and although I got some measure of care in the practical sense, what I also received from the man who should have loved me was pain. Why? Because he cheated on me, he called me names, and his treatment left me bruised in so many ways that human eyes cannot see, but the hurt was sharp and humiliating.

In all honesty, having a baby while I was still a little girl myself brought upon me responsibilities that I was not ready for. Many times I wanted to run away from the situation, but it kept facing me in the hardest ways because a child needs care whether or not you feel ready to be a mother, and in light of this, I had to keep showing up even when my heart wanted to flee. It felt like my whole world was drowning, and I was drowning with it, trying to hold on to anything I could find. Most days, I felt like I was slipping under the water and did not know where to breathe. There were nights when I stared at the ceiling and wondered how I would keep going, and in those moments,

I learned what it means to be tired and to keep going anyway because the little life depending on me could not be put on hold.

You may be reading this and feel something stirring in your heart because you also know what it means to lose school, dreams, friendships, and young freedoms while life drags you into hard work and hard choices. If that is you, then I want you to hear this: "Losing a season of life does not mean losing your whole life, and even when the world seems to have closed a door for you, I want you to know that there are other doors that can open when you are ready to see them. My story did not stop because I left school; it simply turned into a different fight, and that fight taught me things I would not have learned otherwise."

The Mirror, the Questions, and the God I Did Not Know I Needed

When I looked in the mirror during those years, I often did not like the face that looked back at me, and sometimes I was frightened by it because it did not match the child who had laughed so easily. That disconnect made me ask hard questions about who I was and why I had become someone I barely recognized. I had grown up in church with my family, and I knew many of the words and the songs, but I still felt empty because church had been a place of habit rather than a place of meeting God in a way that would change the inside of my life. So, I continued to look for love in people and in choices that only gave me temporary relief.

Many times I wished someone would meet me in the place where I was hurting, yet again and again I convinced myself that no one ever could. That belief left me hollow, because once you begin to think you are beyond help, you will also quietly stop trying to be helped at all. I tried to make the man love me in the way I thought he should, giving more of myself than I ever intended, holding on to the fragile hope that he would stay. But he did not, and the person I had become for the sake of that hope felt discarded, used, and left behind. In those moments, I learned more about loneliness than I ever wanted to know.

Still, here is the turning point I need you to notice. At the very time when hope seemed completely gone, I began to encounter the reality of God's love in a way I had never experienced before. It did not appear like some sudden miracle that erased my pain in an instant, but rather it started coming gently, almost like breathing in truth one breath at a time, until it slowly reshaped the way I saw myself. I did not yet grasp the full greatness of His power, nor did I understand that His love can reach even the most rejected soul and still declare with certainty, "I see you, I love you, and I will not leave you."

When I finally chose to be honest before Him and to ask for His help, my heart began to feel something it had not known in a very long time. There was a peace that no longer depended on what others thought about me.

Lessons I Learned and an Invitation for You

I want to speak to you from my heart because I do not want my story to be only about my past; I want it to be a lantern for you who are walking through a similar darkness. Even before we go deeper in this book, I want you to understand that making a mistake does not make you useless, and being young and lost does not make you beyond repair, because life is full of wrong turns, but God's mercy is always large enough to meet us there.

I want you to ask yourself this honest question right now: where are you looking for love from, and who are you letting shape who you think you are? This question may sting you a bit, and it should, because honest stings have the power to open the way to healing. If you are brave enough to ask God to meet you where you are, then you may find the new beginning I found.

I am not saying it is easy, but I am saying it is always possible, and I am saying this from the place of one who has lived through the fear and the shame and then felt the gentle reclaiming of a life that thought itself finished. If you are carrying sorrow because you had to leave a place you loved, if you are bearing shame from choices made in a season of emptiness, or if the mirror frightens you, then hear me now: you are not beyond help, and you are not beyond being loved.

Your story is not finished at that point where your world felt like it was drowning. This is not just hopeful talk; it is the truth I have lived, and I assure you that the same power that met me can meet you.

What would it mean for you to look into the mirror tomorrow and feel that you are being seen and known rather than scared by what you see? I need you to hold that question with courage and let it lead you as you keep reading because I am here to help you keep going until you begin to live the life you want and need.

THE PAST CAN BE A CHAIN OR A LAMP

The Heavy Weight of Yesterday

There is a truth about life that many people often overlook until it catches up with them in full force, and that truth is that the past never really disappears on its own. It will always linger like a shadow, sometimes waiting for the right moment to speak in your ears or press upon your heart. You see, what you did, what was done to you, and what you failed to do are all stored in memory. Although time may create distance, the weight of yesterday can remain as real as the day it first happened. The reality is that the past has a strange ability to shape how you see yourself, how you see others, and even how you see God. If you do not confront it properly, it can chain you to a life of regret, sorrow, or shame.

The Bible says in Isaiah 43:18-19, *"Remember ye not the former things, neither consider the things of old. Behold, I will do a new thing; now it shall spring forth; shall ye not know it?"* This is not a careless dismissal of memory. It is a powerful call to refuse to let what is behind dictate what is before you. God's voice here is telling us that a person who keeps replaying the scenes of failure, sin, or disappointments that happened in the past will definitely struggle to notice the new thing He is ready to bring forth. The danger of this lies in being so entangled with yesterday that you become unable to even recognize the opportunities of today.

There are people who stumble morally, like young women who fell into sexual sin and bore children outside wedlock, and instead of rising again with dignity, they allowed the whispers of shame to sentence them to a lifetime of self-hatred or even suicidal despair. How about young men who once fell into drugs or crime, and because of that they now believe they can never be more than the mistakes they made? You see, these examples reveal something urgent. They are meant to let you know that if you allow yesterday's failures to define your identity, then your past will become a chain that is cold and unyielding, always dragging you backward until you suffocate under the weight of depression, bitterness, and despair.

But mark my words, the past does not have to be a chain, because the same past can become a lamp that burns with lessons that can illuminate the path of wisdom, humility, and strength for your future.

When the Past Becomes a Chain

There are countless ways in which people allow the past to enslave them, and though the forms may differ, the effect is always the same: they end up with a life that is void of joy, potential, and vision. Some of the ways include:

- **The Chain of Shame:** Shame has the power to attach itself to the deepest part of your memory in such a way that it will take the worst thing you ever did and make it feel like that is the only thing people will ever see in you. Once it sets in, you will begin to believe that you are nothing more than your failure. You will find yourself avoiding church because you do not feel worthy to sit there, you will stop answering calls from friends because you do not want them to see the pain in your eyes, and you will avoid even your own reflection in the mirror because it will begin to feel like the person staring back at you is a stranger. Truly, shame will make you live in the shadow of one mistake as if your entire life can be summed up by it.

- **The Chain of Guilt:** Guilt is something that will never let you rest. It will keep reminding you of what you did wrong and tell you that you must keep paying for it, even when there is nothing left to pay. At first, it may sound like a simple reminder, but before long, it will take over your thoughts until you cannot sleep peacefully, you cannot laugh without feeling fake, and you cannot plan for tomorrow because you still feel tied to yesterday. I tell you, if you are not careful, guilt will convince you that you are unworthy of peace and unworthy of forgiveness. Even if you try to move forward, it will drag you back to the same memory and force you to replay it as though you could change it. In time, you will end up punishing yourself in ways no one else could ever do, and you will keep living under a weight that was never meant to stay on your shoulders.

- **The Chain of Bitterness:** Bitterness comes from real hurt, but it does not stay there; it usually grows into something much larger, and if you do not let go of it, it can begin to shape everything you see and do. When you are bitter, you will hold on to how people wronged you until it colors your conversations, your trust, and even your relationships with those who never hurt you. You will even begin to think that anger makes you strong, but what it really does is lock you inside your pain. You may also begin to push people away without even realizing it, and those who try to love you will feel your distance because you no longer allow yourself to be soft or open.

- **The Chain of Regret:** Regret is another kind of chain that comes from the past. This is a chain that will keep reminding you of what could have been. It will tell you that you should have chosen differently, you should have acted sooner, and because you did not, your life is now damaged beyond repair. I know this firsthand because I have lived it. Regret will keep you living in the past and continually apologizing in your mind to moments that are already gone, as well as make you believe that your future is already wasted. Its goal is to stop you from dreaming, stop you from hoping, and stop you from trying. Let me warn you, the more you listen to regret, the weaker your courage will become in life.

Beloved, when these chains are on you, they will eventually rob you of the will to dream, distort how you see yourself in life, and slowly destroy your confidence in God's mercy. Believe me, nothing is more tragic than to see someone who still has life and opportunity before them living as though their story has already ended in disaster just because they cannot let go of the past.

The Bible warns us in Hebrews 12:15, *"Looking diligently lest any man fail of the grace of God; lest any root of bitterness springing up trouble you, and thereby many be defiled."* I want you to notice how a root of bitterness is described as something that not only troubles the person who carries it but also spreads destruction to others as well. This is exactly how the chains of the past work. They will not stay hidden inside you; sooner or later they spill over into corrupting your relationships, destroying your peace, and robbing you of joy.

Now, let me ask you something: what will you allow your past to do to you? Will you let it tighten around you like a prison chain, or will you decide that its only power is the lesson it leaves behind?

WHEN THE PAST BECOMES A LAMP

On the other side lies a very different possibility. I am talking about the fact that the past can also be your lamp, shining not with condemnation but with clarity. What once brought you pain can give you perspective, what once seemed like the end of your story can stand as proof that you survived, and what once humiliated you can humble you in a way that positions you for greater wisdom.

13

I want you to think of the failures that once broke you. As you do, I want you to know that although they are reminders that you are not invincible, they are also reminders that you are still here. And if you are here, then it means you are not hopeless yet. You can still win.

Think of the wrong turns you took. They may have delayed you, but they also taught you discernment for the journey ahead. When you let the past become a lamp, you will no longer walk blindly into the same traps because your wounds themselves have become your teachers. The Psalmist said in Psalm 119:105, *"Thy word is a lamp unto my feet, and a light unto my path."* Something I quickly need to point out here is that although your past experiences can serve as a guide and lessons, they must always be interpreted through the Word of God. When left alone, memory can deceive, but when filtered through God's Word, even the most painful mistakes can become stepping stones of insight and strength.

- The lamp of the past exposes where pride led to a fall, so that humility can become your guide in the future.
- The lamp of the past reveals where compromise led to pain, so you will learn to guard your convictions.
- The lamp of the past shows where misplaced trust caused betrayal, so that you will begin to discern character with greater care.

At the end of the day, I can assure you that when you see your negative past this way, you will not curse your history, nor will you glorify it. Rather, you will be able to recognize it as part of the divine classroom in which God trains your heart for maturity.

The Choice Between Lamp and Chain

Life will always present you with a decision that no one else can make on your behalf. That decision today is: will your past serve as a lamp, or will it remain a chain? This choice is yours, and it is one of the most defining decisions of your life because no matter what anyone has said, no matter what labels people have tried to stick upon you, you will always remain the one with the authority to decide what role your history will play in your destiny.

Apostle Paul, who knew the weight of a dark past filled with violence and persecution, said in Philippians 3:13-14, *"Brethren, I count not myself to have apprehended: but this one thing I do, forgetting those things which are behind, and reaching forth unto those things which are before, I press toward the mark for the prize of the high calling of God in Christ Jesus."* Did you notice how he frames it? He did not say it as though the past had vanished, but as a deliberate refusal to allow it to dictate his course. His eyes were fixed on the future, and the past was put in its rightful place.

It is time for you to ask yourself honestly: are you pressing forward, or are you still chained backward? Are you using yesterday as a lamp to guide your steps, or as a chain to strangle your soul?

Refuse to Die in Yesterday

The past is powerful, but its power is not absolute because you have been given the right to decide what it becomes in your life. It can remain a chain, weighing you down with shame, guilt, and regret until you wither under despair, or it can rise as a lamp, reminding you of what to avoid, showing you where God's mercy brought you through, and lighting your way toward tomorrow. Always remember that you are not the sum total of your worst mistake, you are not defined forever by the chapter you wish never happened, and you are not condemned to die in yesterday's darkness. The truth is, God has given you the ability to choose, and if you choose life, if you choose hope, if you choose to let the past go, then even the scars of yesterday can shine with the brilliance of grace.

So I challenge you today: do not waste another moment dragging chains that were never meant to be permanent. Lift up the lamp of memory, guided by the Word of God, and step boldly into the future He has already prepared.

CHAPTER TWO

WHEN YOU DON'T KNOW THE LOVE OF GOD AND HIS GREATNESS, YOU KNOW NOTHING

Life Can Be Difficult

At the age of eighteen, I found myself pregnant again for the same man, carrying my second child while still being only a girl trying to figure out who I was and what I wanted in life. My family tried to be there for me, and in their own way, they gave me the support they could, but even with people around, loneliness can sometimes find a way of settling deep into the corners of your heart. I sat at home with two children on my hands, watching my peers take steps into schools, careers, and relationships that seemed so full of promise, and I could not help but wonder what next, what am I going to do with my life, how am I going to find meaning again? The truth is, it was a mess, and no amount of pretending could change that. There were nights when I would look into the mirror and not even recognize myself. The face staring back at me was not the girl I once thought I was going to be. It was someone tired, lost, and confused, and I could not find the strength to love her. Have you ever looked at yourself and felt like you were staring at a stranger, someone you did not want to admit was you? That is where I was. And it was in that place that I began to understand how difficult life can truly become when the weight of circumstances meets the absence of hope.

Life Is Not a Straight Path

In truth, life has never been, and will never be, a straight path without bends, bumps, or unexpected turns. As long as we walk on this earth, we are not perfect beings; we are people who are learning, stumbling, growing, falling short along the way, and constantly walking into perfection. This is why you will make mistakes, and that is why you will sometimes face things that you never thought you would ever have to face, because perfection is not the state of man here on earth. Rather, we are walking toward it, and in that journey, mistakes and difficulties are bound to come.

Sometimes the challenges we face in life are the result of our own mistakes; I mean they are the result of our own poor choices or lack of wisdom. But at other times, they are not ours at all. I am talking about a situation where you suffer because of someone's choices. Let's say, for example, you grew up in a broken home and carried scars from your parents' fights and betrayals you never asked for. Were you the one who told them to choose each other? Of course not. This is what it means to suffer because of the mistakes of others. Also, perhaps you were betrayed by someone you trusted, or maybe you were mistreated by a parent, a boss, or even a pastor. These are things you did not plan, and neither are they your direct mistake, but they can still leave marks on your life, and you cannot deny that they made the road more difficult to walk.

You see, this is what makes life so heavy at times. The challenges and pains of our pasts are not always about your own personal decisions; they can also be the ripple effect of someone else's wrong choice, bad habits, or terrible actions. This is where many people stumble, because instead of learning how to walk through these difficulties of the past with a steady heart, they often let the weight of life crush them. Do you realize how many lives are destroyed not because of the presence of challenges but because of the absence of a deeper anchor during those challenges?

The Danger of Facing Life Without Knowing the Love of God

Beloved, life itself is hard enough even when you have hope, but when you are walking through its storms without knowing the love of God, the weight can become unbearable, and the tragedy of such a life is far more devastating than many are willing to admit. If you are not acquainted with the love and grace of God, what actually happens is that you will become vulnerable to every whisper of the enemy, every reminder of your past, every lie that says you are finished, worthless, and beyond repair. Yes, without the anchor of God's love in your heart, you will always easily collapse under pressures that you would have been able to conquer if you only knew you were loved, cherished, and carried by His grace.

Take a moment to think about this: what do you hold onto when everything else is falling apart? Because everyone will one day face the crushing weight of betrayal, loss, disappointment, or failure, and the real question is not whether life will throw storms at you, but whether you will still stand after the storm has passed. If your anchor is missing, if you are not rooted in the love of God, then you are like a ship tossed by violent waves without any anchor, drifting wherever the current of pain pushes you. That is a dangerous place to live. The Bible gives us countless examples of people who faced life's difficulties, and what separated those who rose from those who fell was whether they knew God's love and trusted His heart for them.

Take a look at the story of Job, for example. He was a man who lost everything, his wealth, his health, and his children, all in what seemed like a blink of an eye. The Bible says in Job 1:20–21, *"Then Job arose, and rent his mantle, and shaved his head, and fell down upon the ground, and worshipped, and said, Naked came I out of my mother's womb, and naked shall I return thither: the LORD gave, and the LORD hath taken away; blessed be the name of the LORD."* Job's circumstances were tragic, but because he knew the faithfulness of God's character, he refused to curse God in his pain. What preserved him was not the absence of difficulty but the presence of faith in God's love and sovereignty.

Now I also want you to imagine what would have happened if Job did not know the love of God. He would have drowned in despair, cursed God, and probably ended his own life. Are you getting it? The difference between Job and many people today is not that his trials were lighter, but that his understanding of God was deeper. This is why the danger of not knowing God's love is so tragic. When you do not know His love, you will interpret suffering as abandonment, interpret trials as punishment, and interpret silence as rejection.

Think also about the children of Israel in the wilderness. Time and again, they faced hunger, thirst, and enemies, and instead of trusting that God loved them enough to provide as He had already done before, they complained, murmured, and even longed to return to Egypt. In Exodus 16:3 they said, *"Would to God we had died by the hand of the LORD in the land of Egypt, when we sat by the flesh pots, and when we did eat bread to the full; for ye have brought us forth into this wilderness, to kill this whole assembly with hunger."* I want you to notice how quickly they misinterpreted their difficulty as evidence that God did not love them. Because they did not rest in His love, every challenge became an accusation against Him, and that is exactly what happens when you do not know the love of God in your own life.

Okay, now imagine someone who has faced a bitter divorce after giving years of sacrifice and loyalty, only to be left broken and discarded. Do you realize that without knowing the love of God, such a person will begin to believe they are unworthy of love, that their life has lost its value, and that there is no reason to hope again? Or think about a parent who loses a child to sickness. Do you realize that without the assurance of God's love, grief can become an endless pit where bitterness against life will grow unchecked, and sometimes anger at God will even begin to consume your soul? These are not just stories; they are the real experiences of many people. Many of them end in despair simply because the people walking through challenges do not know the depth of God's love and grace that can hold them up when they cannot stand on their own.

The Scriptures remind us again and again that God's love is not absent in suffering. Romans 8:35–39 asks, *"Who shall separate us from the love of Christ? shall tribulation, or distress, or persecution, or famine, or nakedness, or peril, or sword? As it is written, For thy sake we are killed all the day long; we are accounted as sheep for the slaughter. Nay, in all these things we are more than conquerors through him that loved us. For I am persuaded, that neither death, nor life, nor angels, nor principalities, nor powers, nor things present, nor things to come, nor height, nor depth, nor any other creature, shall be able to separate us from the love of God, which is in Christ Jesus our Lord."* This means that, regardless of the pain, failure, or betrayal, God's love is not absent. But if you do not know this truth, you will believe every lie that says otherwise.

A Danger to Always Avoid

The danger of not knowing His love is that you will begin to live in bondage to every negative voice. Shame will tell you that your failures are your name; guilt will convince you that you cannot be forgiven;

bitterness will chain you to the wrongs of others; regret will tell you that your best days are gone, and because you do not know God's love, you will believe these voices, let them sit on the throne of your heart, and before long your entire life will become a reflection of lies rather than the truth of God's Word. I want you to think carefully about this: how many people have ended their lives too soon, how many have walked away from marriages, how many have abandoned their faith, not because God was absent, but because they never truly knew His love? Do you see now why this is so tragic? The love was always there, but their ignorance blinded them, and they destroyed themselves carrying burdens they were never meant to carry alone.

You must know that the absence of knowing God's love in your life is not a small matter. It is the difference between despair and hope, between bondage and freedom, between ruin and redemption. Life will be difficult, yes, but it can become unbearable when you do not know that you are loved by the One who has promised never to leave you nor forsake you (Hebrews 13:5). Without that assurance, I can assure you that every storm will become a sentence of death, every failure will become your identity, and every scar can become your destiny. But when you know His love and grace, you will understand that even in the storm, you are not abandoned; even in failure, you are not finished; and even in pain, you are not worthless.

So let me put it plainly, the greatest danger in life is not the storm itself, but walking through the storm without knowing the love and the grace of God. Because more often than not, it is not the storm that destroys people; it is the lie that you are unloved, unseen, hopeless, and unwanted that does. And that is a lie you cannot afford to believe.

You Cannot Let the Past Destroy You

In light of all this, as difficult as life can be, and as real as the pain of the past may feel, it must be clear in your heart that you cannot afford to let the past destroy you. The reason is simple, if you let the past take control, you are surrendering your future to a voice that was never meant to lead you. The reality is that pain will always try to define you, mistakes will always try to label you, and difficult seasons will always try to set the limits of your future through a painful past. But you must decide whether you will accept those lies or allow the light of God's love to shine on them.

When His love shines on your past, it does not erase the events, but it has the power to redefine them, break the sting of shame, and replace it with hope. It will lift you from regret and set your eyes on redemption. However, when you do not know His love, the past will become a prison, and you can become both the prisoner and the guard, replaying your failures and losses as though they are the only truths of your life.

Life is difficult, yes, but it is not unlivable, and you cannot let yesterday's pain convince you that tomorrow is already ruined. You can get past your past by accepting God's love. Lamentations 3:22–23 says, ***"It is of the LORD's mercies that we are not consumed, because his compassions fail not. They are new every morning: great is thy faithfulness."*** That means no matter how heavy yesterday was, there is always the possibility of a new morning when you allow the mercy of God to touch your life.

So I need you to understand this, life is difficult, but true tragedy is when you face that difficulty without knowing the love of God. Your mistakes, your hardships, and your scars do not have to be the end of your story, but if you remain blind to His love, you will keep destroying yourself with guilt and fear.

AN UNVEILING OF THE LOVE AND GRACE OF GOD

God Loves You Unconditionally

As you go through life, I want you to know that there are truths that stand so tall and shine so bright that if you ever allow them to sink into your heart, they will change you forever. One of those truths is this, "God loves you with a love that is not based on your performance, not dependent on your past, and not conditioned by your failures, but rooted in His very nature." The Bible says in 1 John 4:8, *"He that loveth not knoweth not God; for God is love."* Are you getting it? The Word does not simply say that God shows love or that He gives love, though both are true, but it says that God is love. This means everything that He does flows out of that eternal and unchanging nature. I assure you, the reality of God's love is not something that should be treated lightly or casually, it is the very foundation upon which your relationship with Him stands, and if you understand this, then nothing from your past should ever be able to bring you down. His love is so powerful that through it God can take you beyond any limitation that your past wants to bring on you.

Who Began the Love Story

It is very important to understand that you are not the one who began this story of love; it started with Him. In 1 John 4:19 the Bible says, *"We love him, because he first loved us."* What this means is that long before you ever turned to Him, long before you ever thought of seeking Him, He already loved you. Yes, He saw you in your

24

weakness, in your brokenness, in your past, in your sin, and instead of walking away, He drew near because His heart burns with compassion for you. The danger many people fall into is believing that God loves them only when they are doing well, only when they have kept all the rules, and only when they look strong on the outside. But that is a lie.

God's love is not dependent on your ability to measure up. Romans 5:8 says it with power, ***"But God commendeth his love toward us, in that, while we were yet sinners, Christ died for us."*** Do not read it in a rush, go back and meditate on it again. "While we were yet sinners" reveals that His love came to you at your worst, not at your best. In other words, no matter what your past may look like, His love is already extended toward you, and that love is greater than every failure, every regret, every guilt, and every wound you may be carrying today.

Now, let me show you the life of some people who truly unveil this truth more clearly because their stories are truly powerful and will bless you a lot.

David (A Man After God's Own Heart Despite Failure)

David's life is one that truly shocks many people, even believers. This was a man called *"a man after God's own heart"* in 1 Samuel 13:14. Nevertheless, his life was far from spotless. This was the man who wrote psalms of worship that still lift hearts to God today, but he was also the man who fell into grievous sin. I am sure that you probably know the story very well. In 2 Samuel 11, David looked upon Bathsheba, desired her, and committed adultery with her, and when she became pregnant, he tried to cover it up by arranging the death of her husband, Uriah, one of his own loyal soldiers. This was not a small mistake; it was deliberate sin, betrayal, and abuse of power. Surely you would think that such a man would be cast off by God forever. But what actually happened? When Nathan the prophet confronted him, David broke down in repentance, crying out in Psalm 51:10, *"Create in me a clean heart, O God; and renew a right spirit within me."* And instead of rejecting him, God forgave him, restored him, and still fulfilled His covenant promises through him.

This should teach you something very important and let you know that you are not defined by your worst moments when you bring them before God. His love and mercy are deeper than your sin.

Think about this, the very Messiah, the Lord Jesus Christ, came through the lineage of David, the man who had once fallen so far. What does that tell you? It should tell you that God's love does not erase you because of your past, instead, it will redeem you, reshape you, and even work through you in ways you cannot imagine. Trust me on this, if God could still use David, He can surely use you, clean you, give you a better life, reach your heart, and ultimately lift you to the high place of life, no matter what your past may be.

Peter (Restored After Denial)

We also have Peter, the bold disciple who swore he would never deny Christ, but in the hour of testing, he fell three times, denying knowing the Lord. Matthew 26:74–75 records his failure and fall for us to see: *"Then began he to curse and to swear, saying, I know not the man. And immediately the cock crew. And Peter remembered the word of Jesus, which said unto him, Before the cock crow, thou shalt deny me thrice. And he went out, and wept bitterly."* Can you imagine the shame that must have consumed him? To have walked with Jesus for three years, to have seen His miracles and heard His teaching, and then to deny Him in the moment when it mattered most. Many would think that was the end of Peter's calling. But look at what happened after the resurrection. In John 21, Jesus personally restored Peter by asking him three times, *"Lovest thou me?"* and with each affirmation, He recommissions him to feed His sheep. What you need to note here is that Jesus did not discard Peter because of his failure in the past. Instead, He reaffirmed his place and entrusted him with the responsibility of leading others. Yes, he had a past that was truly tragic. But Jesus had to let him know that his commission was still in view and that his past had not destroyed him.

This is the beauty of God's love: it not only forgives, it restores, it not only wipes away the past, it breathes new purpose into the future. And at the end of the day, Peter went on to become a mighty preacher of the gospel, standing boldly on the day of Pentecost in Acts 2 and declaring the very Christ he had once denied. What changed? It was the encounter with the unconditional love and grace of the Lord that lifted him from the shame of his past into a life of boldness and victory. The same can happen to you if you will allow God today.

JESUS AND THE WOMAN CAUGHT IN ADULTERY

There are few places in the Bible where the heart of God's love and grace is revealed more tenderly than in John 8, where the scribes and Pharisees brought to Jesus a woman caught in adultery. According to the Law of Moses, she should have been stoned, so they threw her in front of the crowd, not out of zeal for righteousness but in an attempt to trap Jesus, forgetting that their scheme would cause the death of this dear woman. What this implies is that her past was so bad and so tragic that it was about to cost her life. Have you ever been in such a situation? The Bible says in John 8:6, *"This they said, tempting him, that they might have to accuse him. But Jesus stooped down, and with his finger wrote on the ground, as though he heard them not."* When they continued pressing Him, He rose and gave an unforgettable reply in John 8:7: *"He that is without sin among you, let him first cast a stone at her."* One by one, her accusers left, until only Jesus was standing there with her. Then He asked in verse 10, *"Woman, where are those thine accusers? hath no man condemned thee?"* And she answered, *"No man, Lord."* To which He then replied, *"Neither do I condemn thee: go, and sin no more."*

Do you see it? The very one who had every right to judge her chose instead to cover her with grace. He did not ignore her sin, but He did not define her by it either. He lifted her from shame, lifted her from the pit, and lifted her from her past and offered her a new beginning. That is the very heart of God's love. You are not condemned by Him because of your past. Romans 8:1 says, *"There is therefore now no condemnation to them which are in Christ Jesus, who walk not after the flesh, but after the Spirit."* Let me tell you this, if Jesus could look at that woman in her most humiliating moment and say, *"Neither do I condemn thee,"* then He can look at you in your brokenness, your mistakes, your secret regrets, your past, and declare the same. His love is greater than your guilt, His grace is stronger than your shame, and His mercy is more faithful than your failures.

Why You Must Accept His Love

The unveiling of this love and grace demands a response from you because it is not enough to merely know that God loves you, you must accept it, embrace it, and let it penetrate the deepest places of your heart. Many people keep God's love at a distance, as though it were meant for others but not for them. You will see them live bound by guilt and always striving to earn His favor, never realizing that His favor was already given through Christ so their past should never hold them back. Ephesians 2:4–5 says, *"But God, who is rich in mercy, for his great love wherewith he loved us, even when we were dead in sins, hath quickened us together with Christ, (by grace ye are saved)."* Do you grasp what this means? Even when you were spiritually dead, even when you had nothing to offer, His love and grace were already reaching toward you, bringing you to life in Christ.

This is why you must not let your past or your present struggles keep you from receiving His love. The truth is, the enemy will try to tell you that you are too far gone, that you have made too many mistakes, and that God could never use you. But know this, those are lies. God's love and grace are relentless, and He will never give up on you. Jeremiah 31:3 puts it this way: *"Yea, I have loved thee with an everlasting love: therefore with lovingkindness have I drawn thee."*

When you accept this love, everything will change and you will begin to see yourself not as the world has labeled you, not as your failures have defined you, but as God sees you, redeemed, beloved, chosen, and forgiven. His love will give you peace in place of turmoil, confidence in place of fear, and hope in place of despair.

The Call to Respond

A major challenge of my life back then was that I did not know that God loves me so deeply and cares for me so much. So, the question remains: will you receive His love today? Will you stop trying to earn what has already been freely given? Will you believe the testimony of Scripture that says in Romans 10:9, *"That if thou shalt confess with thy mouth the Lord Jesus, and shalt believe in thine heart that God hath raised him from the dead, thou shalt be saved"*? This is not a religious ritual and not an empty tradition, it is the very doorway into the reality of God's love so you can experience a transformed life.

Do not push this truth aside and do not think it is for someone else. God's love is personal and it is for you. The stories of David, Peter, and the woman caught in adultery are not ancient tales of distant people, they are living testimonies letting us know that God's heart is always to redeem, to restore, and to embrace you.

Believe me when I tell you this, you will never find a greater truth to build your life upon than the love and grace of God revealed in Jesus Christ. It is unconditional, it is unshakable, and it is unending. It will pursue you in your darkest valley, lift you in your deepest pit, and restore you when you think all hope is lost. All you need to do is receive it, hold it close, and let it change you from the inside out.

CHAPTER THREE

THE LOVE OF GOD MAKES A DIFFERENCE

You Are Fearfully and Wonderfully Made

I did not always know or even believe that I was fearfully and wonderfully made because there were days when all I could see about myself was pain, rejection, and a deep sense of not being enough. I remember nights when I cried myself to sleep, confused about why life had turned the way it did and questioning whether I had any value left at all. I carried wounds that no one could see and scars that went beyond the surface, and because of this, I believed the lies told to my mind by situations, that maybe I was worthless, maybe I had failed too badly, and maybe there was nothing about me worth living for. But in the midst of all those moments, the love of God was silently holding me together, and I did not even realize it at first. However, today I can boldly tell you that the love of God is what always makes the difference.

You see, when David wrote in the Psalms, *"I will praise thee; for I am fearfully and wonderfully made: marvellous are thy works; and that my soul knoweth right well"* (Psalm 139:14 KJV), he was not simply speaking about a casual truth; he was unveiling the reality of God's intentional care and design for every one of us. Even in those moments when I felt like nothing, when I thought I had been abandoned, and when my heart was torn into pieces because of what my supposed husband was doing, God's Word was always saying something entirely different about me. His Word was always that I am wonderfully and fearfully made. Made with reverence, with wonder, and with purpose. As far as God is concerned, you and I are always marvelous, no matter what your past may be saying.

That alone changes everything because when you truly see yourself through the lens of God's love, you will understand that your value never came from people, from relationships, or from circumstances; it comes from God Himself, the One who formed you with His own hands and declared you precious. There were days when I could not stop replaying the pain in my mind, when the betrayal made me feel like I was not good enough, and when rejection left me wandering inside my own thoughts, walking and talking to myself, feeling as if I might lose my mind and go crazy. This was so terrible that sleepless nights became normal, and my heart was weighed down by a kind of loneliness so heavy that I thought I would be crushed beneath it.

But then, even in those darkest nights, I began to realize something. I was still standing, I had not lost my mind, and I was still alive. And that in itself was not an accident. It was proof that God was keeping me, that His love was carrying me when I could not carry myself, and that His grace was surrounding me even when I thought I was forgotten. That is why I can stand today and tell anyone who cares to listen that the love of God can make the difference for you if you will allow Him. It was His love that kept me from breaking completely and His love that reminded me that I was fearfully and wonderfully made.

Life will always try to convince you otherwise. People will tell you that you are not good enough, society will look down on you, and even your own mistakes and past will scream loudly in your ears, saying you are a failure. But God's voice is stronger, and His Word speaks louder if only you can choose to listen. Psalm 139 does not only say we are fearfully and wonderfully made, it also reveals that God's thoughts toward you are precious and so many that they outnumber the grains of sand. That means when I was thinking I was unloved and forgotten, God was constantly thinking about me with love, with care, and with an eternal plan for my life. And the truth is, He is thinking the same about you too.

So when you look back at those pasts of yours, I want you to begin to see them through the lens of God's love, and I can say with confidence that none of it can destroy you because His hands are holding you all the way. The love of God made the difference in my story, and it will make the difference in yours, too.

God's Thoughts Toward You Are Precious

The Psalm goes further in verses 17 and 18, saying: ***"How precious also are thy thoughts unto me, O God! how great is the sum of them! If I should count them, they are more in number than the sand: when I awake, I am still with thee."*** Can you take note of how powerful this is? God's thoughts toward you are not occasional or casual; they are precious and beyond number. That means while people may reject you, belittle you, or replace you because of your past, God will never stop thinking about you with love and care.

Think about that for a moment. The very One who created heaven and earth thinks of you continually, not with anger or condemnation, but with love, compassion, and a plan for your good. When I felt I had lost everything, this truth was always there, and if only I had known it, it would have healed me much earlier. Today, it can heal you. It may be instant, but you have to realize that even if the world dismisses you, God's thoughts toward you will always remain precious. This is true. You are not defined by past mistakes or the opinions of others; you are defined by the love of God, a love I have been saying to you can make the difference in your worth and identity.

These are some of the reasons why you must never allow society or circumstances to dictate your value. People may call you worthless, but the Word of God calls you wonderful. People may say you are a failure, but the Word says you are marvelous. People may say you are forgotten, but God's thoughts about you are countless as the sand. And when you finally choose to see yourself through His love, everything changes.

God's Power Can Help You If You Trust Him

I know what it feels like to long for love, to desperately hope someone will see you as worthy, and to be left empty when that love does not last. That emptiness can be crushing, and society has a way of making it worse because people will say you are no good, that you will never measure up, and that your future is already ruined. But in the middle of that despair, here is a truth I want you to hold on to: "God's power can help you if you trust Him." Yes, He can!

The Bible says in Jeremiah 29:11, ***"For I know the thoughts that I think toward you, saith the Lord, thoughts of peace, and not of evil, to give you an expected end."*** God's plan for your life is not destruction; it is peace. His desire is not to abandon you but to give you hope and a future. When you put your trust in Him, His power will begin to work in your heart, healing broken places, giving you strength you never thought you had, and lifting you above the labels society tries to place on you.

The woman we discussed earlier in John 8 is another great example of this. According to the law, she deserved to be stoned, and everyone around her was ready to condemn and destroy her. But what did Jesus do? He said, *"He that is without sin among you, let him first cast a stone at her"* (John 8:7), and one by one, her accusers left. Finally, Jesus said to her, *"Neither do I condemn thee: go, and sin no more"* (John 8:11 KJV). This is the difference the love of God makes. It can take someone society has labeled, someone who is broken and ashamed, and restore them with grace and compassion. He offered her freedom, hope, and a new beginning, and that is exactly what He is offering you from your past right now.

If you are currently thinking that your past is shameful, I want you to meditate on this woman's story. It should remind you that no matter what others said or are saying about you, and no matter the mistakes or errors you may have made in the past, Jesus is not standing with stones in His hands to condemn you. Instead, He is offering you forgiveness, healing, and purpose. That is what happens when you trust Him. His power lifts you above condemnation and sets you free to live again.

So to you reading this, I want you to know that even if society looks down on you, even if people have rejected you, and even if your own heart is heavy with shame, the love of God can still make a difference in your life. Trust Him because His power will help you carry burdens you cannot carry on your own, and His grace will silence every voice that says you are worthless.

God's Power Meets You in Your Weakness

You may feel like you do not have the ability to do anything meaningful, and I understand that feeling because I once believed the same about myself. I thought my failures and rejections had stripped me of every possibility. But I have now learned something about God. He delights in showing His strength through our weakness. His Word says in 2 Corinthians 12:9, *"My grace is sufficient for thee: for my strength is made perfect in weakness."* This means you do not have to be strong on your own because when you admit your weakness and trust Him, His power becomes visible in your life.

Think of Gideon, hiding in fear from the Midianites, convinced he was the least in his family and unfit for greatness. In that weakness, God called him a *"mighty man of valour"* (Judges 6:12) and used him to deliver Israel. The lesson here is that your limitations and past do not disqualify you from God's plan. In fact, they are the very places where His power wants to shine.

Trust Him today so He can take the labels society has put on you and replace them with His promises. Where they say you are useless, He says you are chosen. Where they say you are finished, He says you have a future. Where they say you are broken, He says you are redeemed. That is the transforming power of God's love over your life.

Perhaps you are a teenager searching for love, longing for someone to notice you, and feeling like nobody cares. Hear me clearly: there is One who sees you, loves you, and calls you complete in Him. Colossians 2:10 says, *"And ye are complete in him, which is the head of all principality and power."* You do not have to keep chasing after people to fill the emptiness in your heart because only Jesus can truly complete you.

Yes, there will be nights when you feel alone, there will be moments when the pain seems unbearable, and there will be times when society tells you that you are no good. But in those very moments, remember that God loves you, and His love does not just comfort; it empowers, lifts, and sets you on a path where your life can become a testimony of His grace.

Jesus Sees You and He Cares

Maybe you are at a point in your life where you feel like giving up. You may even be thinking that your life is not worth living anymore. Perhaps you have been abused, betrayed, or hurt so deeply that you feel dirty and broken. Maybe even your parents have turned their backs on you. You may feel unloved, unwanted, and alone. It could be that you thought you had finally found love, only for that person to take away the little hope and self-worth you had left, and now it feels like you have nothing and you are convinced your life is a mess. I know how that feels because I have been there myself. I tried to hold on to anything that could make me feel valuable, and I even went to church, but deep inside I was still empty, still looking for love, and still searching for meaning in my life.

Take note of this. The Bible says, *"The Lord is near to those who have a broken heart, and saves such as have a contrite spirit"* (Psalm 34:18, NKJV). That means you are not abandoned, even when everyone else walks away. God will never leave you. He comes closer when you are hurting, and He is not ashamed of your pain. He is not repelled by your tears or your past. Instead, He will always bend down to meet you right where you are.

The Bible also says, *"You number my wanderings; put my tears into Your bottle; are they not in Your book?"* (Psalm 56:8, NKJV). What I need you to know is that every tear you have cried, every sleepless night you have endured, every moment of pain you thought no one saw, God has seen all of it. He has kept records of your sorrow because your life matters to Him. Jesus Himself said, *"Come to Me, all you who labor and are heavy laden, and I will give you rest"* (Matthew 11:28, NKJV). He was speaking directly to people like you and me, people who are tired, worn out, and broken down by life, and He has promised not to turn you away. In fact, right now, He is inviting you to lay down the heavy load you are carrying so that He can give you peace.

He Will Not Leave You Alone

When you feel like nobody cares, I want you to remember what God says: *"Fear not, for I am with you; be not dismayed, for I am your God. I will strengthen you, yes, I will help you, I will uphold you with My righteous right hand"* (Isaiah 41:10, NKJV). You never have to walk through this battle alone. God Himself is saying that He will hold you up. Even in the darkest valley, He has not left you. You may feel surrounded by despair, but the Shepherd is walking right beside you, and He is closer than you think.

The pain you are facing right now is not the end of your story because God has a way of taking what is broken and making it whole again. He promises to give us beauty for ashes, the oil of joy for mourning, and the garment of praise for the spirit of heaviness (Isaiah 61:3,

NKJV). That is what He wants to do for you. You may feel like nothing good can come from your life, but God is able to restore what was lost and what others thought was destroyed. God can bring it back with greater purpose.

CHAPTER FOUR

ONLY GOD'S LOVE CAN HEAL YOUR BROKEN HEART

Have you ever sat in silence, wondering if anyone truly sees the tears you cry when no one else is around, or if anyone could ever truly understand the weight on your shoulders? Maybe you have carried pain for so long that right now it is beginning to feel like a part of your identity, or maybe you have convinced yourself that no one would even care if you ever spoke about it. Well, in all honesty, you do not have to keep quiet anymore, and you do not have to carry the pain alone because only God's love can heal your broken heart, and I mean it with every fiber of my being.

Romans 5:8 says, *"But God commendeth his love toward us, in that, while we were yet sinners, Christ died for us."* Like I said before, the love of God is not waiting until you are perfect, nor until you are free from mistakes, nor until you finally have your life together before it falls on you. No, the Bible says even a man still in error is worthy of His love. This is God's love coming right into your brokenness, into your shame, and into the very moment you thought you were least deserving of it. It is because of how beautiful such love is that I can tell you to begin to speak today. Yes, begin to tell Jesus everything, because He longs to hear, and He understands everything you are passing through. You see, silence only gives your pain more power, but prayer releases it into hands stronger than yours. When you tell the Lord what you have never dared to say aloud to anyone, the Lord will bend low to listen.

1 John 3:1 says, *"Behold, what manner of love the Father hath bestowed upon us, that we should be called the sons of God."* Can

you just imagine that? You are a child of God. You are not forgotten, not abandoned, and not worthless. You are His child, and His children are never meant to carry wounds in secret.

So I say to you, do not keep quiet. Begin to talk today. If you have been crying behind closed doors, let those same lips begin to speak to God, and if you have been sinking under the weight of shame, start laying it down in His presence. I am simply saying, tell Him the story of your hurt, tell Him the words you never told your parents, tell Him about the betrayal, the rejection, the abuse, and the loneliness because He already knows, yet He wants you to pour it out on Him so He can take it off your heart and off your life completely. The moment you begin to open up to Him, something will shift in your life. It may not erase your past overnight, but it will release you from its prison.

God's Love Does Not Fail Even When People Do

I know the sting of human love when it turns cold, the ache of promises when they are broken, and the bitterness of rejection when it makes you question your worth. Perhaps you too have been there, convinced that you were finally safe in someone's arms, only to discover that they never valued you as much as you thought. I know how painful such wounds can feel, not because I read about it in a book, but because I have been through that terrible experience.

But here is the reality: you must understand that the love of people, no matter how sincere it looks in the moment, is never the final measure of your worth. Human love fails, but the love of God never does. The Bible says in Isaiah 49:15-16, *"Can a woman forget her sucking child, that she should not have compassion on the son of her womb? yea, they may forget, yet will I not forget thee. Behold, I have graven thee upon the palms of my hands."* Yes, that is true. Even if the very one who birthed you can forget, God says He will not. This is truly an amazing love, and this is why it has the power to mend broken souls, heal broken hearts, and restore shattered lives.

Beloved, you must never base your value on the actions of people who walked away from you because they did not create you, they did not breathe life into you, they did not design the purpose within you, and they certainly do not have the final say over your life and destiny. Only God does. And His verdict is love. I am talking about an unchanging, unrelenting, and undeniable love. When I remember the nights I cried myself to sleep, wishing I could be good enough for someone who had already replaced me in his heart, I cannot help but acknowledge the fact that it was God who kept me through those seasons.

It is possible that there is a challenge in your life right now, and you are between the choice of giving up or holding on. Know this: you do not have to give up. If you can trust in God's love, that love will always be enough to carry you through, even when every human being has failed to love you as you expected them to.

Give Him the Pain You Have Been Carrying

You do not have to bear the weight of your past alone, and you do not have to carry the shame that has followed you like a shadow. 1 Peter 5:7 says you should cast your cares on Him: *"Casting all your care upon him; for he careth for you."* God is not asking you to hide your pain. He is inviting you to hand it over to Him. Psalm 147:3 says, *"He healeth the broken in heart, and bindeth up their wounds."* I assure you, that pain in your heart and that regret about the past, He can handle it better than you are doing right now. I know it may feel difficult because sometimes pain can become so familiar that you may almost cling to it as though it were a part of your identity. Nevertheless, your pain is not who you are, and your wounds do not define you. God's word does, and He says you are His beloved, wonderfully and fearfully made to be special, amazing, and glorious.

You should take a moment to imagine what it means to actually let go, to open your hands and say, "Lord, here it is, every wound, every memory, every disappointment, every secret I thought would bury me." When you release it to Him, He will receive it not with disgust and not with condemnation, but with compassion. The psalmist said in Psalm 34:18, *"The Lord is nigh unto them that are of a broken heart; and saveth such as be of a contrite spirit."* In other words, the very thing you thought would disqualify you is the very thing that draws His presence nearer. And let me emphasize this again: God is not repelled by your pain; He is drawn to it. He is not overwhelmed by your brokenness; He is the only one able to heal it. That is why you must give Him the pain you have been carrying.

- Give Him the loneliness that suffocates you at night.
- Give Him the betrayal that still burns like a fresh wound.
- Give Him the shame that whispers you are not good enough.
- Give Him the fear that convinces you tomorrow will not be better.

You are to lay it all down at His feet.

Love That Lays Down Its Life

When Jesus spoke to His disciples in John 15:13 KJV, He said, *"Greater love hath no man than this, that a man lay down his life for his friends."* That was not just a teaching; it was a declaration of what He was about to do. On the cross, He laid down His life not because you were strong, but because you were weak; not because you were worthy, but because you were loved. And today, that love has not expired. The cross is not just a past event; it is still a very present reality, and every time you doubt your worth, you need only look to Calvary and remember that someone thought you were worth dying for. Not just someone, Jesus Christ, the Son of God.

Your brokenness does not intimidate Him, your mistakes do not disqualify you, and your tears do not push Him away. On the contrary, they are a reminder of why He came. He came to heal the brokenhearted, to bind up the wounds, and to set the captives free. He said in Luke 4:18, *"The Spirit of the Lord is upon me, because he hath anointed me to preach the gospel to the poor; he hath sent me to heal the brokenhearted, to preach deliverance to the captives, and recovering of sight to the blind, to set at liberty them that are bruised."* Are you getting it? His mission was never about the perfect, the polished, or the ones who had it all together. It was always about people like you and me, the ones who feel like giving up, the ones who have been broken, and the ones who cannot imagine being whole again because He wants to heal all our broken hearts with His love.

In light of all I have said, let me say it one more time: you do not have to keep quiet anymore. Begin to talk today and start telling Jesus everything you have held back because He is waiting to take what is too heavy for you. You may feel trapped, you may feel unloved, you may feel worthless, but believe me when I tell you that the cross is the proof that you are worth everything to Him.

Remember Psalm 147:3 KJV, *"He healeth the broken in heart, and bindeth up their wounds."* This promise is not for someone else; it is for you. Take it, believe it, and walk in it.

CHAPTER FIVE

THE SHOCK AFTER THE TEEN YEARS

When I Thought It Was All Over

I thought the worst was behind me after my teenage years, because who would believe life could bring more pain than what I had already walked through, but then the shock that came later nearly destroyed me. I soon met a man I thought was great. When I met him, everything looked good on the surface; he seemed steady, responsible, and like someone who could give me the space to breathe as well as shower me with the love I had always longed for. I never knew that he was broken on the inside, carrying pain and hurts. Soon enough, we started a relationship, we worked together, and we built a business, and in that beginning, I held onto the hope that our mutual needs might meet and heal. I wanted someone to love me and to hold the place in my heart that had been torn, and I thought he wanted the same. But, painfully speaking, I was very wrong!

Of course, there were some red flags, but then I was probably desperate for belonging, and I ignored them, thinking maybe love could be enough to bridge our gaps.

As I was saying, when we met it seemed too good to be true, but I did not know that his heart had been broken too or that he was carrying bitterness that hurt. He was trying to find someone to love and to fill an empty space inside him, and I was looking for someone to love me and to heal my broken heart. I never knew that I was looking to the wrong source and the wrong place. At the end of the day, our different worlds collided, and I did not see it coming.

Our business grew and did well, and soon people started to like me a lot, and everything seemed alright from the outside. We then started a house together. I worked so hard day and night so things would get better, because I wanted the life we would build to be a place of peace and belonging.

The Business, the House, and the Falling Apart

At a certain point in time, it seemed like all heck broke loose in my life, because if I talked with people it became a problem, and if I did anything at all, it would always seem to offend him. How could life get so miserable? He soon started to curse and to call me things I had never imagined. Truly, I did not even know I could go through so much. And once again, many nights I cried myself to sleep. He became so insecure, and every day started feeling as though I was living in a nightmare. And guess what, each day it got worse.

In fact, I ran away many times, thinking I could get away from him, but wherever I went, he found me. Sometimes he cursed me so badly that people in the area would gather to hear what was taking place. I would be so ashamed when I walked on the street and passed people; I would just hang my head in shame. A time came when I once again began to wonder if it was worth living like this. Trust me, I went through every abuse you can think of: sexual, verbal, mental, emotional, and even physical. This man was crazy in the ways he behaved. Sometimes I felt like a slave, working so hard and finding no rest. Many nights I cried, asking myself what have I done in life that I am going through all these things? Sometimes I would pretend everything was alright, but my heart was crying out for help.

In fact, I went on daily doing what I should do, ignoring what was taking place in my life, wondering if it was really happening and whether it would change someday so that I could feel love, joy, and happiness again. All these were constantly on my mind, all at the same time.

I also felt lonely more and more as days, weeks, months, and years went by. I did not know where to turn, and although I earnestly desired and longed to experience the kind of happiness I heard people talk about, it just seemed like God was not answering me.

The Darkest Hours and the Small Voice

A time came when I reached a point where I wanted to kill this man and commit suicide to end the misery as well. I say it plainly because it is the truth and because the depth of my despair must be told exactly as it was felt. But there was a small voice speaking to me not to do it. That voice stopped me. I do not have another name for it; I only know what it did.

Nevertheless, as time went by, I continually grew bitter, hated myself, hated the man, hated the world, and hated everyone who came around me. Over the years, I continued working, having a house but not calling it a home, because a home is where love and happiness are found, and as for mine, it had none. Every time I ran away he found me and begged me to come back, saying things were going to get better, but instead, it often got worse.

I did not have anyone to contact. I felt dirty, no good, shameful, without self-worth, and looked down on by society. When I passed on the street people laughed at me; I was so ashamed. I was also afraid that if I told anyone, he could kill me. At the end of the day, I was consistently living with a deep and ever-present pain in my soul, which expressed itself in certain acts of suicidal thoughts and a paralyzing fear that controlled my very breath.

Years went by and the suffering continued. It was not for a single moment but a long, slow, and painful one. I would always ask myself, do I have to live like this? Is this my life now? Those questions were fierce, and they demanded answers I did not yet have the courage to find.

The Shift That Started Changing Everything

As years went by, something in me shifted when I began to visit church more regularly. At first, it was a routine I kept because I had nowhere else to place my hope, but later it became a place where I felt the presence of God in small but steady ways, so I decided that my life could not keep going on like this.

While attending a convention at the church one day, the pastor asked for prayer requests, so I wrote mine on a piece of paper, asking God that if He would deliver me out of that situation, I would serve Him. The pastor also said, you must believe God for what you are asking for. Well, I believed because I was desperate for deliverance. From that day, I began to know that God was a miracle-working God because He answered my prayers. I do not write this lightly; I write it as a fact. God moved! He answered! He began to pull me out step by step.

I am telling you all this now because it is all behind me, and because I want you, as you read these words, to know that there is a way through that tunnel of pain and past hurts that you have been suffering with in your life. I no longer carry that load; the misery is in the past, and I am sharing what happened with you in the hope of encouraging those who may be where I once was. There is no glorifying the pain and no making it pretty. It happened exactly as I have been telling you, but the fact that it happened does not mean it has the last word or say over my life. It is not in the past, and I have risen above it because I accepted God and His love into my life.

Do you remember that small voice I spoke of? It was one of the turning points God used to help me. Maybe you have felt that whisper too, or maybe you have been held back from the worst by something you cannot explain. I want you to hold on to that. It is real, and it is mercy by the grace of God reaching out to you.

My Heart to You

I want to say clearly to anyone who hears this, the years I lived through that pain taught me about the cruelty people can carry, but they also taught me that God is near to the broken and that deliverance can come when you are desperate enough to reach for it. I was ashamed, I was humiliated, I felt looked down upon by society, and I was afraid to even tell my family, but God met me in the place of my secrecy and answered the cry I wrote on a scrap of paper. As you read the story of my life, I want you to take a good examination of yours also.

You may be asking, does this mean everything changed the moment I prayed? No. The change came in time, in small steps, and in answers that were sometimes quiet and sometimes obvious. I stayed working, I kept the household running, and I kept praying and trusting God. If you will stay with God, then I want you to know that your story is not finished yet. In fact, it is only just beginning, and God is set to do great wonders through your life.

ENCOUNTERING GOD'S LOVE IN THE MIDST OF LONELINESS

When Salvation Does Not Seem to Answer Every Question

When I first gave my life to Christ, I truly thought everything would immediately fall into place, and I believed that my struggles would end the very moment I said yes to Him. I was convinced that all I needed was that single step, and from there, my life would automatically blossom into beauty without any lingering ache of the past. But the reality, as I soon discovered, was different. I was saved, yes, and I do not doubt that the Lord had brought me out of darkness into His marvelous light, yet there was still something within me that longed to be affirmed, something that cried out for someone to look at me and say, "You are special, you are loved, you matter."

Something I quickly need to say here is that you should not make the mistake of thinking that salvation means you will never wrestle with the hunger for certain desires or even affection again. It does not really work that way. The truth is, salvation will not erase your human need for connection, but rather redirects you to the one place where true fulfillment can be found, and that is in God Himself. If you keep expecting people to constantly validate you, then you will always be disappointed because people are limited, but God's love is limitless. The Word of God says in 1 John 3:1, ***"Behold, what manner of love the Father hath bestowed upon us, that we should be called the sons of God."*** You have to know that God is not just tolerating us; He has bestowed His love upon us.

So, even though I had been saved, I was still searching for someone to make me feel valuable, and as I searched, I always realized that not everyone I looked to was willing or even able to fill that gap. Most people were too busy carrying their own burdens.

Nights of Tears and an Encounter with God

Even after coming through the heavy hurts of my past and entering into a new chapter of life in Christ, I expected to finally find ease. Yet there were days when I still found myself lonely and empty, and nights when I lay in bed with tears soaking my pillow, crying silently so no one would hear. Beloved, you must never allow loneliness to drive you to the wrong arms and never let your hunger for love push you into the traps of the enemy because the devil is a master at exploiting desperate hearts. He will tell lies into your ears, tell you that you need to compromise, that you need to accept less than God's best, and that you need to cling to people who will only use and discard you. But I assure you, nothing could be further from the truth. In Romans 5:8, God has already given you the highest love, and the proof of that love is the eternal sacrifice of Christ on the cross.

One night, as I cried and wrestled with many questions, I had an encounter with God that changed me. In the stillness, I heard His voice speak to me so clearly, calling me by name. He said, "You are special to Me, I have called you, You are Mine." Friend, believe me, that night marked a turning point in my life. For the first time, the truth of God's personal love for me moved from my head into my heart. Indeed, it was truly a glorious night. Maybe right now you are reading this and feel the same ache I once felt, and maybe you are wondering if anyone really sees you or values you. I am here to tell you that God sees you, He knows your name, and He has called you His own. Colossians 1:13

says, *"Who hath delivered us from the power of darkness, and hath translated us into the kingdom of his dear Son."* This is not a distant promise; it is your reality if you believe.

Laying Down the Heavy Burdens

From that moment onward, I realized that no matter how bad my situation looked, there was always an invitation waiting for me at the feet of Jesus. The Bible says in Matthew 11:28–30, *"Come unto me, all ye that labour and are heavy laden, and I will give you rest. Take my yoke upon you, and learn of me; for I am meek and lowly in heart: and ye shall find rest unto your souls. For my yoke is easy, and my burden is light."* These words should become a lifeline for you. I discovered that I did not have to carry the weight of my past or my pain alone. Pause with me here, and let me ask you, how long will you keep struggling with burdens that Christ has already offered to carry for you? How long will you keep holding on to grief, shame, and loneliness as though they are treasures instead of chains? Believe me, the sooner you lay them down at His feet, the sooner you will know true rest.

I soon realized that my tears, my regrets, and my feelings of worthlessness were never too heavy for God. There is no problem so great that He cannot solve it, no grief so deep that He cannot comfort it, and no past so stained that He cannot wash it clean. What people often fail to understand is that love is not just an emotion; it is an action, and the greatest demonstration of love is what Jesus Christ did on the cross. This is why He could boldly say to us, "Greater love hath no man than this, that a man lay down his life for his friends." It is time for you to stop measuring love by feelings alone and start measuring it by truth because feelings will always change, but God's Word will stand forever.

Rising Above the Lies of the Enemy

Is it not amazing that even after I had a life-changing encounter with God's love, the enemy did not stop attacking me? In fact, I noticed that the devil often tried to bring up my past, planting memories of pain and failure in my mind, hoping I would accept them as my identity. This is what I call mental oppression, the enemy telling you, "You are still the same person, you will never rise above this, and you are unworthy of God's love." But here's the thing: you do not have to accept every thought that enters your mind. The Bible says in 2 Corinthians 10:5, *"Casting down imaginations, and every high thing that exalteth itself against the knowledge of God, and bringing into captivity every thought to the obedience of Christ."* This means that you have the authority to reject the devil's lies and to hold fast to God's truth.

Let me caution you right here: if you keep entertaining the enemy's whispers, they will grow louder until they drown out God's voice in your spirit. But if you choose daily to fill your heart and mind with the Word of God, then you will find strength and stability even when the storms of memory come back to fight you. It is like feeling as Jeremiah did in the dungeon when he was surrounded by mire with no way out. Lamentations 3:21–23 is a strong pillar of hope if this is where you are right now. The Bible says, *"This I recall to my mind, therefore have I hope. It is of the LORD's mercies that we are not consumed, because his compassions fail not. They are new every morning: great is thy faithfulness."* No matter how deep your pit seems, there is hope, because God's mercies are new every single morning.

CHAPTER SIX

FINDING PEACE IN THE MIDST OF LIFE'S STORMS

When Fear Drowns Out Faith

Have you ever stopped to wonder why Jesus looked at His disciples in the boat, when the waves were crashing and the storm was raging, and said, *"How is it that ye have no faith?"* (Mark 4:40). The truth is, they were not alone; Jesus was right there with them, yet their fear blinded them to His presence. What this means is that they allowed the sound of the wind and the sight of the waves to make them forget that the One who calms storms was right there in their midst. Tragically, this is exactly how many of us live today. The moment the storms of life rise up, the moment things begin to shake, we also begin to panic as though God has abandoned us, when in reality He has never left us for one moment. We lose sight of His promises, and we allow fear to take the driver's seat of our hearts. Fear of rejection, fear of loneliness, fear of sickness, fear of failure, even fear of death. These fears often become dark shadows that envelope our minds until we are imprisoned inside ourselves.

My counsel to you is that you must not allow fear to control your mind anymore because fear will always exaggerate the problem and minimize your faith. Fear will tell you lies that God has forgotten you, when His Word has already promised in Hebrews 13:5, *"I will never leave thee, nor forsake thee."* If Jesus is on board with you, then I want you to know that you may feel the winds, you may hear the thunder, but you will not sink. The Psalmist said in Psalm 46:1 that God is our refuge and strength, a very present help in trouble. Do you understand? He is not a distant help, not a delayed help, but a very present help. That means in the exact moment the storm is raging, God is right there, closer than your next breath, and He will never let you drown. I urge you today, do not run from God when the storm comes. Too many believers, when trouble arises, withdraw from church, from prayer, and even from the very presence of God, where their strength lies. You will hear them say things like, "I just need a break," when what they truly need is to run into the arms of God. The worst thing you can do in a storm is to disconnect from the anchor that keeps you steady.

The Battle Between Fear and Peace

There is a peace available to you that no storm can steal, but the question is, are you holding on to it? Jesus said in John 14:27, *"Peace I leave with you, my peace I give unto you: not as the world giveth, give I unto you. Let not your heart be troubled, neither let it be afraid."* Take note of the words, *"Let not your heart be troubled."* That means you have a choice. Fear is always waiting at the door of your heart, but you must decide not to open it. Without the Word of God, there can be no peace. Why? Peace is rooted in knowing and believing His promises. If you let go of His Word, your peace will slip through your fingers. Do not forget that fear thrives in the absence of faith, and faith only comes by hearing the Word of God (Romans 10:17). Are you seeing why you must fill your heart daily with His Word? Every time the enemy comes with fear, you can stand your ground with truth.

Think about Psalm 27:1, which says, *"The LORD is my light and my salvation; whom shall I fear? the LORD is the strength of my life; of whom shall I be afraid?"* This verse alone can silence every fear if you let it settle into your heart. No matter what, do not ever spend so much time thinking about what you must do that you neglect who you have been called to be. Sometimes we are so consumed with activity, with solving problems, and with trying to manage every detail of life that we soon forget the most important truth: we are children of God. And if we are children, then we are loved, secured, and protected by Him. Identity must always come before activity, because when you know who you are, you will know how to live.

Yes, it is time for you to stop letting daily busyness crowd out your spiritual growth, and stop letting your service for God become a substitute for intimacy with God, because the storms of life will always expose whether you are standing on the solid rock of His presence or on the fragile ground of your own strength. If you are standing in your own strength, then you will fail again and again, and your past will keep swallowing you.

The God Who Heals Broken Hearts

Today I want to tell you that no matter how deep your pain is, no matter how shattered your heart feels, Jesus is able to heal you completely. The prophet Isaiah foretold of Him in Isaiah 61:1: ***"The Spirit of the Lord GOD is upon me; because the LORD hath anointed me to preach good tidings unto the meek; he hath sent me to bind up the brokenhearted, to proclaim liberty to the captives, and the opening of the prison to them that are bound."*** Maybe you have been through a relationship that left you wounded, used, and discarded. Maybe you trusted someone with your heart, only for them to treat you like a doormat, calling you names, cursing you, and tearing down your self-worth. Maybe you kept begging them to love you while inside you felt worthless, ashamed, and unloved. Perhaps your story is even darker and more terrible, like mine, because you gave your youth to someone who promised love but gave you betrayal. You sacrificed your schooling, your dreams, and even bore a child thinking it would secure affection, only to find yourself abandoned and bitter.

If that is you, I need you to hear me clearly: your life does not end there. The love of Jesus is higher, deeper, and wider than every betrayal you have faced. You do not have to let the bitterness of the past define your future because God's love is the healing balm that can restore every shattered piece of your heart. Do not give up on love just because people failed you. Do not close yourself in bitterness, hating yourself and everything around you. The place that hurts the most is the exact place God wants to fill with His love. He is not intimidated by your scars, He is not repelled by your brokenness, and He is not ashamed of your tears. He is still here, waiting to receive you.

Look at Psalm 34:18 again: *"The LORD is nigh unto them that are of a broken heart; and saveth such as be of a contrite spirit."* If your heart is broken in two, if you feel like life is no longer worth living, if you do not know where to turn, then turn to Jesus. Tell Him your pain, tell Him your bitterness, tell Him your loneliness, and tell Him your fears, because He understands everything you are going through.

Even as you are reading, do not harden your heart as God is speaking to you. Let go of that past! Hebrews 3:15 says, *"Today if ye will hear his voice, harden not your hearts."* Every storm is an invitation to draw closer to Him, so do not stiffen your neck and run from His love, but yield and let Him lift you out of despair and out of that terrible past.

- When you feel abandoned, remember He said, *"I will not leave you comfortless: I will come to you"* (John 14:18).
- When you feel unloved, remember, *"Yea, I have loved thee with an everlasting love: therefore with lovingkindness have I drawn thee"* (Jeremiah 31:3).
- When you feel broken, remember, *"He healeth the broken in heart, and bindeth up their wounds"* (Psalm 147:3).

Jesus Christ is the same yesterday, today, and forever. If He calmed the storm for His disciples, He can calm the storm in your life. If He healed the brokenhearted in Scripture, He can heal yours today and redeem your past.

RESTING IN GOD'S UNCHANGING LOVE

Only God's Love Makes the Difference

There comes a point in every life when you must face the reality that nothing in this world has the power to truly satisfy, heal, and restore except the love of God. I can assure you, and I stand by this with every fiber of my being, that it is only the love of God that makes the real difference in life, as we have discussed in a previous chapter. Human affection may comfort you for a moment, riches may bring you some fleeting relief, and achievements may even give a temporary sense of value, but none of these things can penetrate the deep wounds of the soul or fill the aching void in the human heart. That is why the Bible reminds us in John 3:16, ***"For God so loved the world, that he gave his only begotten Son, that whosoever believeth in him should not perish, but have everlasting life."*** You see, what God offers us in His love is not just words of comfort, but a complete and unchanging embrace that meets us at the very core of our brokenness. When He gave His Son upon the cross, He was not offering a shallow expression of care; He was giving Himself fully and without reservation, so that no matter what pain or rejection we may endure in this life, we would have a constant assurance that we are loved with a love that cannot be taken away.

There were times in my own life when tears clouded my vision, and I felt as though I had no strength left to stand. However, I have learned that if I could just lift my eyes beyond the pain, beyond the confusion, and fix them on the loving face of Jesus, there I would find hope. He has never been too busy to hear my cry. He has never turned me away when I came to Him broken and weary. And I know this same love is reaching out to you even now, because God is always our refuge and strength, a very present help in trouble. He is not far off, not distant, but right there with you.

When Challenges Rise Against Your Peace

Satan will always do all that he can to challenge your peace. He will try to disturb your happiness, always bring back your past that you are trying to forget, and he will continually tempt you to doubt whether God is truly with you. But beloved, you must rest and know that God does not change. He is the same yesterday, today, and forever, and if He has promised never to leave you nor forsake you, then you can be confident that He will remain faithful no matter what comes your way and no matter what your past may be saying. When Jesus said in John 14:27, *"Peace I leave with you, and my peace I give unto you,"* He was not joking or playing games with you. This also means that not even your past or any other thing has the right to steal your peace and joy. The enemy wants you to live bound in fear, trapped in anxiety, and consumed by hopelessness, but the Word of God gives you authority to stand against those lies. Fear may tell you that your life is over, but faith should always rise in your heart and tell you that your steps are ordered by the Lord. Fear may suggest that nothing will ever change, but faith should respond in you and say with Psalm 37:5, *"Commit thy way unto the Lord; trust also in him; and he shall bring it to pass."*

These are some of the things I have had to learn personally. There were moments when fear pressed so hard on my spirit that it felt like a weight I could not lift. I questioned whether I could survive certain trials, and the uncertainty nearly consumed me. Yet when I determined in my heart that no matter how bad things appeared, I would continue to pray and hold on to God's promises, something remarkable happened. His peace, the very peace Jesus spoke of, began to guard my heart. It did not mean the problems vanished instantly, but it meant I could walk through them without being destroyed by them. That, my friend, is the power of God's love at work.

My Mother's Passing and God's Presence

Let me share a part of my story that proves this truth beyond words. There came a time when my mother fell seriously ill. The doctors diagnosed her with cancer, and after she was hospitalized, they told us plainly that there was no hope. I cannot describe the weight that fell on me in that moment. I felt helpless, and in many ways, I did not know where to turn. But one thing I did know was that God was with me, even in that valley. A few weeks later, my mother passed away. I loved her dearly, and losing her was not something I could prepare my heart for. Yet something so amazing, something beyond human explanation, took place within me. In that time when I should have been broken beyond repair, I found peace. It was not the kind of peace the world offers with shallow words or quick distractions, but a deep and abiding calm that came from God's love surrounding me every single day. I did not feel the unbearable pain I expected, and though I grieved, I was not consumed by sorrow. Instead, I felt as though His presence was wrapping itself around me like a protective shield.

Psalm 34:18 is truly a powerful scripture. I can say I lived that scripture. God Himself carried me through that storm, and though I had lost both my father and now my mother, He never left me to face life alone. His love kept me, His peace sustained me, and His presence became more real than ever before. Believe me when I say that if I had not accepted the love of God, I do not know how I would have made it through such loss. But because His love was dwelling within me, I could stand, I could continue, and I could testify that God is indeed faithful.

Strength in the Midst of My Son's Trouble

Not long after, I was faced with another storm that shook me deeply. I received the news that my son had gotten into serious trouble, and the pain of it nearly broke me. I cannot put into words the heaviness that filled my heart when we got that news. It felt as though all hope was gone, and I was left beaten down, weak, and utterly forsaken. There were nights I lay awake wondering how I would make it through another day, and there were moments when I felt as though God Himself had turned His back on me.

But then I remembered the story of Job, who, despite losing everything, never gave up his trust in God. I thought of how the Lord had carried me through the loss of my mother, and I reminded myself that if He had been faithful then, He would not fail me now. I purposed in my heart that I would not give up, no matter how hopeless the situation appeared. And so, I prayed. I prayed with tears, I prayed with groanings, and I prayed even when I did not see an immediate answer.

As I applied the Word of God to my life daily, strength began to rise in me again. It was not my own strength, because on my own I had none left, but it was the strength that came from knowing that the God who promised to be with me was still in control. Psalm 37:23 says, ***"The steps of a good man are ordered by the Lord: and he delighteth in his way."*** I clung to that verse, and I trusted that even though my son's path seemed lost, God could order his steps and bring restoration.

And here's the thing: God did not just give me endurance, He comforted me in the midst of my sorrow. The only true source of happiness I could find in that season was in Him. The fear did come, the darkness tried to overwhelm me, but each time I cried out to Him, He reminded me that my tears were not in vain, He was strengthening me, and He was working even when I could not see it.

CHAPTER SEVEN

THE POWER OF GOD'S LOVE IN THE FACE OF LIFE'S AND YOUR PAST

My Mother's Passing and God's Presence

As I mentioned earlier about my mother dying from cancer, I can still clearly remember going to church that very night because our church was having a crusade and the choir was going to sing. I was a part of the choir, and I decided that nothing was going to stop me from singing. My heart was broken, but I still said to myself, "Lorna, you will still sing to the Lord."

While I was there, I heard the voice of the Lord say to me, "Lorna, worship Me." I recognized it was God talking to me, so I said, "God, my mother just died, and You are telling me to bow down and worship?" It did not make sense to my mind, but something inside me knew that this was not the time to run away, it was the time to draw near. You know, I was in so much pain because I loved my mother dearly, the grief was fresh, and my chest was heavy, but I found myself bending down on my knees on the ground, worshiping God with my whole heart. That was an experience I will never forget! It felt like surrender and strength met together, and in that moment of obedience, God began to show me that He truly was always present in the middle of any adversity, no matter what I may be going through.

Because my son needed a lawyer for certain things at that time, the little money I had was gone, but that very night, God showed up for me, and He provided the money I could use to go to Jamaica to help bury my mother. What a mighty God we serve! Indeed, He is a great

God! The pain was real, the battle was tough, and I had no plan for victory, but God had already gone ahead of me.

Another challenge that stood before me at that time was the legal fees needed for my son's case. It was about two million for court hearings. I did not have a husband to lean on or a partner to split the burden with. But I did have Jehovah Jireh, the God who provides. Step by step, with the help of my family and God's unexpected provision, the bills were paid. Each payment became a testimony, and each obstacle a reminder that I was not alone.

I am telling you this not to repeat a sad story but to show you the nature of God. He is not only an ever-present help but also an all-knowing Father who cares about our needs. We often wish we could escape troubles, pain, grief, loss, and the frustrations that wear us down, but the promise of God is not that we will avoid storms, it is that He will be with us in the storm and His presence will always be our source of power, courage, and wisdom to navigate the difficult times.

What I need you to learn from this season of life is that when trouble comes, our natural instinct is to get worked up, confused, or distracted, and sometimes even frustrated with God. But the key is humility, admitting that you need His help and thanking Him for being by your side even when you may not feel it. I assure you that problems will arise and circumstances will continue to change, but God will always remain constant. He does not break His promises, He does not change His nature, and He will never abandon us as His children.

I have also realized that tough times expose what you really believe about God. When things seem like they are falling apart, you have a choice, you can either let bitterness grow or you can hold fast to your faith. Do you not know that believing in Jesus as Lord and Savior does not mean you will never cry? However, it does mean that even while you are crying, you can have confidence that He is working. That is what I did in those days, I chose to wait, to endure, to stay connected, and not to let anything steal my joy or distract me from His voice.

From that experience, look at three powerful lessons about overcoming adversity by relying on God:

1. **Worship shifts the atmosphere of your heart:** It does not erase the pain, but it lifts you above it. When you worship, you are telling your soul that God is bigger than the problem. That shift opens your heart to receive peace and guidance.
2. **Provision flows where faith is active:** I did not see God's provision until I acted on faith, showing up at the crusade, singing in the choir, and kneeling on the floor. When I gave Him my pain, He gave me His supply.
3. **God's presence is the true comforter:** People may mean well, but I want you to know that only God can hold the invisible parts of your soul, and when you lean on Him, He will carry not only the practical burdens but also the emotional ones.

I know as you read this, you may be going through your own version of loss or lack. Maybe it is not a parent's death but a broken marriage, a betrayal, or a financial crisis. Perhaps you too are asking, "God, how can You expect me to worship in this pain?" Let my life testify to you that worship is not a denial of pain, it is rather a doorway into God's strength because when you worship in the midst of your pain, you are inviting God to meet you in the ashes and to begin building beauty again.

GOD'S LOVE GIVES YOU THE FOUNDATION FOR VICTORY

As a believer, when you truly become rooted in God's love, I mean when you have the love of God in your heart, you should know that you are not empty or lacking in any way. His love has the power to fill every void and establishes you with a foundation that cannot be shaken. That is a reason why, as much as I can, I always encourage everyone within my reach that no matter where they come from or what they may have faced or are facing, they should always accept the love of God in their lives and begin to live by it. This is because when you have His love, then you truly have everything you will ever need in life. You may not have wealth, you may not have prestige, you may not even have all the answers to the struggles and challenges you are going through, but if you have God's love, then you have the greatest treasure of all. His love is an assurance that the Almighty is with you, He will fight your battles, and He will never abandon you.

According to Psalm 46:1, the Bible does not say that God was our help or He will be our help in some distant future, but that He is a present help right now, that is, in this very moment. When storms are raging around you, you do not have to crumble under the weight of fear, because you can be confident that God has sovereignty over all things. He is omnipotent, and this means He is all-powerful. He is omniscient, meaning He knows all things, and He is omnipresent, meaning He is present everywhere at the same time. When you begin to rest in these truths, you will discover that there is no challenge too great for Him to handle and no storm too violent for Him to calm.

And let me tell you this, you will also be able to face both your past and current challenges with confidence, power, and resilience until you conquer. There is no escaping this reality. But then I also need you to know that there are some challenges that will come into your life, God may permit them, nevertheless, you should also know that they were never designed to destroy you. Rather, they are only permitted to shape you, to strengthen you, and to teach you to lean more fully on Him. Hence, James 1:2-3 says, *"My brethren, count it all joy when ye fall into divers temptations; Knowing this, that the trying of your faith worketh patience."* You see, trials are not wasted experiences; they are the very places where God demonstrates His power and builds your faith.

Rising Above the Storms of Life

There is something remarkable we can learn from the eagle, because while other birds scatter and hide when a storm comes, the eagle does something entirely different, it uses the storm to rise higher. Instead of being defeated by the winds, the eagle spreads its wings and allows those very winds to lift it above the clouds where the storm can no longer touch it. In the same way, God is calling you and me not to run from the storms of life, but to face them with courage, knowing that with His strength, we can soar higher through them.

Isaiah 40:31 declares, *"But they that wait upon the LORD shall renew their strength; they shall mount up with wings as eagles; they shall run, and not be weary; and they shall walk, and not faint."* This scripture is giving us a clear picture of what it means to rise above challenges. You see, your storms are not meant to bury you, they are meant to lift you. But the key is learning to wait upon the Lord, to trust Him in the waiting, and to lean on His everlasting arms.

At certain periods of my own life when I faced what seemed like impossible situations, I mean times when I had no money to pay rent, no means to put food on the table, and no way to provide for my children. The weight of those days could have crushed me, but instead of giving in to despair, I cried out to God, and time after time, He proved Himself faithful by making a way where there seemed to be no way, and He reminded me that my provision does not come from man, but from Him. Psalm 23:1 became more than just words on a page, it became a living reality for me. *"The LORD is my shepherd; I shall not want."*

I can guarantee you that when you put your trust in Him, you too will see His hand moving in ways you cannot explain. He delights in providing for His children. Psalm 37:25 says, *"I have been young, and now am old; yet have I not seen the righteous forsaken, nor his seed begging bread."* Believe me when I say this, He will not forsake you.

Learning to Carry Your Cross and Finish the Race

One of the greatest mistakes we often make is comparing our journey to someone else's, wishing we had their strength, their blessings, or even their challenges, instead of recognizing that God has given us our own cross to bear. Whatever challenge comes your way, it is not by accident. God has only permitted it for a reason, and rather than running from it or despising it, you must ask Him for grace to carry it, because His grace is sufficient for you. Jesus Himself told us in Matthew 16:24 that *"If any man will come after me, let him deny himself, and take up his cross, and follow me."* In other words, following Christ will always involve sacrifice, and it will always involve carrying a cross. But here is the good news, your cross will never be more than you can bear with His help, and it is always meant to lead you closer to Him.

I have come to realize that the race of faith is not about how you start, it is about how you finish. God did not save you just to begin the race, He saved you so that you can endure to the end. Hebrews 12:1 puts it this way, *"Let us run with patience the race that is set before us."* Patience is needed because the race is long and filled with obstacles, but when you set your eyes on Jesus, the author and finisher of your faith, you will not faint.

Challenges are not always punishments, sometimes they are promotions in disguise. And when God allows pressure in your life, it is because He wants to bring something greater out of you. Just as gold is refined by fire, your faith is strengthened by trials. And when you come out on the other side, you will realize that what you thought was meant to break you was actually the very thing that lifted you higher in your walk with God.

PRAYING THROUGH CHALLENGES AND STANDING ON GOD'S PROMISES

Okay, let us talk about one of the major weapons that God has provided to sustain us through every challenge: prayer. I have said it again and again that you cannot face the storms of life in your own strength; you need the strength that comes from crying out to God in prayer and standing on His promises. Look at Philippians 4:6-7, *"Be careful for nothing; but in every thing by prayer and supplication with thanksgiving let your requests be made known unto God. And the peace of God, which passeth all understanding, shall keep your hearts and minds through Christ Jesus."* Prayer is not just a ritual, it is your lifeline and your connection to heaven. It is the place where you are able to exchange your weakness for God's strength, your sorrow for His joy, and your fear for His peace. And when you combine prayer with faith in God's Word, you become unshakable in every way. Ephesians 6:16 puts it this way, *"Above all, taking the shield of faith, wherewith ye shall be able to quench all the fiery darts of the wicked."*

There were many times when I had to fall on my knees, sometimes weeping, sometimes too weary to even find the words, but in those moments, I discovered that Jesus was closer than ever whenever I opened my mouth and called on Him. He is never too busy to hear your cry, and He will never walk away from you when you need Him most. Psalm 91:11 is another scripture of great comfort: *"For he shall give his angels charge over thee, to keep thee in all thy ways."*

You must never allow your tears to drown you, but rather let those tears drive you to prayer. Stop the weeping and start trusting. Expect your miracle and live boldly. Take a look at Psalm 118:6: *"The LORD is on my side; I will not fear: what can man do unto me?"* Isn't this amazing? When you pray, when you trust, and when you stand on the promises of God, you will rise above every challenge, and you will find the strength to keep pressing forward.

LIVING IN THE POWER OF GOD'S WORD

Strengthened Through Christ's Power

The reality is that life will always present seasons that challenge your strength, shake your confidence, and tempt you to give in to fear. But then, the Word of God says something entirely different about who you are and what you can do when Christ lives in you. Paul, writing in Philippians 4:13, makes a bold declaration saying, *"I can do all things through Christ which strengtheneth me."* This verse is not a shallow statement of motivation; it is the very foundation upon which your ability to rise above the failures of your past rests. When you rely on your own human strength, it has limits because the flesh and willpower can carry you only so far before they collapse under pressure, but when you tap into the strength of Christ, there is a flow of power that will sustain you in ways that cannot be explained by human reasoning.

And make no mistake, this strength is not just for extraordinary occasions but for everyday living, for the temptations you face, for the fear that tries to choke your faith, for the uncertainty of tomorrow, and even for the memories of yesterday that are trying to chain you down. You can stand boldly and say, "Yes, I failed before, but that failure does not define me, because I can do all things through Christ." You better believe this, the power of Christ is available to equip you not only to endure but to overcome. The world may have counted you out, people may have written your name off, and circumstances may have tried to bury you in shame, but the strength of Jesus Christ can lift you beyond all of that and set your feet on solid ground if you will allow Him.

Paul also prayed in Colossians 1:11 that believers might be *"strengthened with all might, according to his glorious power, unto all patience and longsuffering with joyfulness."* I want you to notice how the strength of God is not only about external victory but also about internal stability. It will give you patience when the waiting feels long, endurance when the battle feels heavy, and joy when everything around you suggests sorrow. This strength can carry you from weakness into courage, from despair into hope, and from your past into your future.

Do not look at yourself as weak, incapable, or unworthy of rising again. Stand in the assurance of Philippians 4:13, lift your head, and declare that you can do all things, not because of your past, not because of your resources, not because of your intellect, but because Christ strengthens you daily with His glorious power. I understand how you may be feeling right now; trust me, I have been there and I have seen the fire of such hell, but I can also tell you that the God who brought me out is set to do the same for you.

The Peace That Guards the Heart

The goal of the enemy has never been to target your body or your finances alone. Often, the first thing he will target is your peace. He knows that when your peace is gone, your mind will easily be enslaved by fear and worry, and the moment that happens, you will be defeated in more ways than you can count, even if you try to fight back.

The Word of God gives us a clear instruction in Colossians 3:15, and I want you to look at it: *"And let the peace of God rule in your hearts, to the which also ye are called in one body; and be ye thankful."* That word *"rule"* is not passive; it means to act as an umpire, a governor, and a ruler who decides what enters and what is expelled. You see, peace is not simply a feeling that visits once in a while, it is a ruling authority given by God to dominate your heart if you allow it. And I need you to understand this, when you accept God's peace, you are refusing to surrender your mind to worry, because worry is nothing more than fear dressed up as concern. It will drain your energy, steal your focus, and magnify your problems until they seem larger than God. But peace does the opposite. Peace will shrink the size of your problems by magnifying the presence of God, steady your thoughts, and remind you that God is still in control, even when the storm rages.

Psalm 23 gives us a perfect picture of this peace. Look at it: *"Yea, though I walk through the valley of the shadow of death, I will fear no evil: for thou art with me; thy rod and thy staff they comfort me."* I need you to notice the wording, it is a valley of the *shadow* of death, not death itself. The shadow of something can never destroy you because it has no substance, and that is exactly what your past is. It has no substance. Fear thrives on shadows, illusions, and threats, but peace will always remind you of the truth that God is with you, His rod and staff are there to guide you, and therefore you have nothing to fear.

So let peace rule in your heart. Do not allow fear of the future, memories of the past, or challenges of the present to dictate how you live. Instead, anchor your mind in God's promises and you will see that peace is not the absence of storms but the presence of Christ within the storm. This is the reason Jesus could sleep in the boat while the storm raged, and that same peace is available to you right now.

Delivered and Preserved by the Lord

Another great assurance you have as a child of God is that He not only strengthens and gives peace but also delivers and preserves. Psalm 37:40 says, *"And the LORD shall help them, and deliver them: he shall deliver them from the wicked, and save them, because they trust in him."* This scripture places the responsibility of deliverance squarely on God, not on you. Isn't that a good thing? Yes, it is. Your role is trust, His role is deliverance.

There are forces, schemes, and devices of the enemy that you may never see with your eyes, but Psalm 33:10 says, ***"The LORD bringeth the counsel of the heathen to nought: he maketh the devices of the people of none effect."*** You may not always know the plans that were made against you, but God cancels them before they can even reach your door. You may not always see the arrows that were shot in the dark, but God makes them of no effect before they strike. You may not always perceive the traps laid before your feet, but God causes them to collapse under the weight of His power. It is in light of this that trust is so vital. Trusting God is not just a spiritual cliché, it is the only lifeline that can keep you safe when danger lurks unseen and when the challenges of both the past and the future come raging at you. And guess what? The Lord does not deliver halfway. He always delivers completely. He will not only bring you out of the cage of your past and present situations, He will also preserve you after bringing you out. Psalm 91:7 tells us that ***"A thousand shall fall at thy side, and ten thousand at thy right hand; but it shall not come nigh thee."*** This is divine preservation at work. Destruction may rage around you, chaos may surround you, but it will not touch you because the hand of the Lord is covering you.

Take it from me, this is not theory, this is reality. God has a track record of protecting His people through the worst of storms and delivering them from terrible pasts, and He will not start failing with you.

Rising in the Spirit's Power

At the very core of overcoming your past and pressing forward into victory lies the power of the Spirit of God. It is not by human strength, not by cleverness, and not by sheer determination that you will ever be able to achieve anything reasonable. Zechariah 4:6 tells us, ***"Not by might, nor by power, but by my spirit, saith the LORD of hosts."*** What this means is that your victory is not manufactured by your effort, it is supplied by God's Spirit working in and through you. If you realize this, then you will know that nothing has the right to put you down, pull you down, or make you live a broken life. It does not matter whether it is from the future, the past, or the present.

Look at 2 Samuel 22:37–38, where David was speaking: ***"Thou hast enlarged my steps under me; so that my feet did not slip. I have pursued mine enemies, and destroyed them; and turned not again until I had consumed them."*** This is what happens when the Spirit of God empowers you. Your steps are enlarged, your footing is steady, and you are able to easily overcome enemies that once seemed impossible to defeat. The Spirit of God will give you courage to confront what once terrified you and strength to stand firm where you once stumbled.

This power also carries with it a promise of victory that is absolute. Psalm 91 assures us that no matter how overwhelming the numbers appear, ***"A thousand shall fall at thy side, and ten thousand at thy right hand; but it shall not come nigh thee."*** The Spirit of God will place a covering over your life that no enemy can penetrate, no weapon can destroy, and no curse can overturn. And yes, it does not matter whether it is an event from your past or present.

Getting past your past is not about trying harder, it is about surrendering deeper. It is about yielding your weakness to the Spirit and allowing Him to clothe you with power. It is about letting go of self-reliance and embracing Spirit-reliance. When you walk in the Spirit, you will not just survive, you will thrive, you will soar above storms like the eagle, and you will be able to walk through fire without being burned.

So remember this, your past cannot hold you, your enemies cannot defeat you, and your fears cannot imprison you when you live in the power of the Spirit. Rise boldly, live fully, and walk daily in the Spirit's strength, because in Him you are more than a conqueror.

CHAPTER EIGHT

YOU CAN LIVE A JOYFUL LIFE

The True Meaning of Joy

What does it really mean to live a joyful life? Is joy the same as happiness, or is it something deeper, stronger, and more enduring than the temporary waves of emotion that often come and go with the changing seasons of life? Happiness is often tied to circumstances because people tend to feel happy when things are working in their favor and when the path before them is smooth, but joy is something greater, something divine, and something unshakable. Joy comes from God Himself and not from fleeting conditions. Know this, joy is not a fragile feeling that depends on your bank account, your relationships, or your physical health. Happiness is what falls into that category. Joy is a spiritual state anchored in the unchanging nature of God, and it is the reason Apostle Paul could write from a prison cell, *"Rejoice in the Lord alway: and again I say, Rejoice"* (Philippians 4:4 KJV).

When you look at the word of God, you will see that joy is a constant theme. David, even in the midst of battles, declared, *"The Lord is my rock, and my fortress, and my deliverer; my God, my strength, in whom I will trust; my buckler, and the horn of my salvation, and my high tower"* (Psalm 18:2 KJV). Can you see that his joy was not rooted in whether the battle was fierce or whether his enemies were many, but in the assurance that God was his strength and his refuge. This shows us that true joy is not the absence of problems but the presence of God in the middle of those problems. When you truly understand joy, you will begin to see that it is God's will for you to live above despairs. It is not His plan that you live under the weight of constant tears, endless pain, and unbearable suffering. Of course, hardships will come, and you will sometimes walk through valleys that seem dark, but that does not mean you are sentenced to a life of sorrow. God's word is clear that He is your strength, your comfort, and your salvation, and He has already guaranteed that you can live with joy. Let me ask you a question: why do so many believers live as though sadness is their permanent portion when God has already given us promises that shout otherwise? Could it be that you have allowed your past to deceive you into thinking that your future is bound to be filled with the same tears? I need you to understand today that your past is not the master of your destiny. God is.

Joy Is God's Guarantee, Not Your Guesswork

If you are going to embrace a joyful life, you must settle this truth in your heart that joy is not a wish or a vague hope, it is a guarantee sealed by God Himself. Do you remember what we read in 2 Samuel 22:33–34 earlier? This is God telling you that your footing in life is secure, not because of your skill or your effort, but because God Himself is the one who lifts you, strengthens you, and plants you firmly where He wants you to stand. The problem is that many people treat joy as if it is a luxury, something for special people or special seasons, but I assure you, joy is your inheritance as a child of God, and not even your past experiences, mistakes, or errors have the right to take it from you. Think about it. Would a loving Father ever design a future for His children that is filled only with unrelenting sorrow? Absolutely not. Psalm 71:21 says, ***"Thou shalt increase my greatness, and comfort me on every side."*** That is God's promise, and when God promises comfort, He does not mean comfort on just one side of your life, He means on every side.

If God has already declared that He will comfort you, why would you resign yourself to despair? Why would you allow yesterday's failures to convince you that joy cannot be your portion today? It is time for you to be intentional about rejecting the lie that says your tears are permanent. That lie is not in line with the Word of God.

- Joy is not tied to your circumstances but to your covenant with God.
- Joy is not a passing feeling but a permanent possession.
- Joy is not for a chosen few but for all who belong to Christ.
- Joy is not fragile because it is anchored in God's unchanging promises.

So I ask you again, will you accept what the world and your past say about your life, or will you accept what God has already guaranteed?

The Strength of Joy in the Midst of Battles

Let me take you a step further because it is not enough to say joy is yours without showing why joy matters so much, especially when life presses you. The Bible lets us know that joy is not just a beautiful gift, it is also a weapon and a strength that can enable you to endure as well as overcome. Nehemiah 8:10 puts it this way, ***"…for the joy of the Lord is your strength."*** Your strength does not come from mere motivation or positive thinking but from the joy that God Himself imparts into your heart. David knew this truth well, because in Psalm 18:39 he said, "thou hast girded me with strength unto the battle, thou hast subdued under me those that rose up against me." What does this tell us? It tells us that joy is not passive, it is active. Joy equips you, joy sustains you, joy gives you courage to stand when others would have fallen.

Think about the apostle Paul again. He was beaten, imprisoned, rejected, and yet still writing about rejoicing. How is that possible? The reality is that joy made him unbreakable. Joy kept him praising when chains were on his hands, and it was that same joy that shook prison doors and set captives free (Acts 16:25–26).

I want to challenge you to reflect on this. When storms rise in your own life, do you collapse under their weight, or do you stand firm because your strength is drawn from the joy of the Lord? And if God has already given you this joy, what excuse can you truly hold on to for living without it?

Joy is not just something you feel once in a while, it is something you must deliberately choose to walk in every day of your life. It is a spiritual discipline as much as it is a spiritual gift.

You see, your past may whisper that joy is not for you, your present struggles may suggest that happiness is impossible, but your faith must rise up and declare, *"God is for me"* (Psalm 56:9). And when you begin to live this way, your joy becomes unstoppable.

Ask yourself these questions:

- What voices have I allowed to convince me that joy is not my portion?
- What would my life look like if I truly believed God's guarantee of joy?
- Am I living as though joy is a fragile feeling, or am I walking as though joy is a permanent gift?

The truth is, every time you declare God's Word, every time you choose to believe rather than fear, every time you thank Him even in the valley, you are choosing joy. And the more you choose it, the stronger it becomes until it becomes your very lifestyle. In 2 Corinthians 10:4–5, the Bible says, *"(For the weapons of our warfare are not carnal, but mighty through God to the pulling down of strong holds;) casting down imaginations, and every high thing that exalteth itself against the knowledge of God, and bringing into captivity every thought to the obedience of Christ."* Joy is one of our weapons, and it is not weak; it is a mighty weapon.

PRACTICAL STEPS FOR WALKING IN JOY EVERY DAY

God has made it possible for you to live with joy, not just once in a while but every single day. This kind of joy is not about pretending that pain does not exist; it is about choosing God's perspective in the middle of the pain so that His joy is then able to swallow the pain and fill your heart with true peace and laughter. The Bible declares, *"He only is my rock and my salvation: he is my defense; I shall not be moved"* (Psalm 62:6 KJV).

Like I said before, it is not automatic; you must learn how to walk in it daily and choose it deliberately. The reality is that sorrow will always try to knock on your door, but you do not have to give it a seat in your living room. Let me now walk you through several practical steps you can take to remain joyful, not just when the sun is shining and everything is going right, but also when the storm rages, when your past is trying to taunt you, or when the present feels unbearable.

- **Begin Each Day Anchored in God's Presence**

This is the first practical thing you can do to walk in joy every day. You must start your day with God rather than with your worries. Too many people roll out of bed, and the first thing they do is check their phones, read the bad news, or rehearse all their troubles in their minds, and then they wonder why they feel drained before the day even begins. But notice what David said in Psalm 5:3, that his voice shall God hear in the morning. And he goes further to say, "O Lord, in the morning will I direct my prayer unto thee, and will look up." Joy begins when you lift your eyes upward instead of inward. Take time to pray, to thank God for keeping you, and to confess His promises over your day. Even a few minutes of genuine fellowship with God can shift the atmosphere of your entire day.

Ask yourself this: if the first voice I hear in the morning is God's, will I not be better equipped to handle the other voices that come later?

• Guard Your Thoughts Like a Treasure

Something else that makes a tremendous difference is learning to control your thoughts. This is very important because the battle for joy is often fought in the mind. Your past will try to replay its ugly scenes, the present will always try to magnify its pains, but you must not allow your mind to wander wherever it wants. 2 Corinthians 10:5 says you should cast down imaginations, and every high thing that exalts itself against the knowledge of God. In other words, you have the authority, through Christ, to decide what stays in your mind and what gets cast out.

When a painful memory surfaces, do not dwell on it endlessly; instead, speak God's Word out loud and replace that thought with His truth. When the present feels like hell, remind yourself of the promises that God has made. For example, you can meditate on *"Thou shalt increase my greatness, and comfort me on every side"* (Psalm 71:21).

84

Joy does not come from ignoring thoughts; it comes from replacing them with God's truth.

- **Speak Joy into Your Day**

Do not underestimate the power of your words, because Proverbs 18:21 says, ***"Death and life are in the power of the tongue."*** What you speak has a way of shaping what you feel, and if all you say are words of defeat, sorrow, and hopelessness, you will live in the shadow of those words. But if you speak life, you will be able to create an atmosphere of joy even in difficulty.

Every morning, declare things like:

- *"The joy of the Lord is my strength"* (Nehemiah 8:10).
- *"God is my rock and my fortress; I shall not be moved"* (Psalm 62:6).
- *"This is the day which the Lord hath made; we will rejoice and be glad in it"* (Psalm 118:24).

When you speak like this, you are not denying reality; you are aligning yourself with God's higher reality. We will discuss this more in the coming chapter, and you will be amazed.

- **Refuse to Isolate Yourself**

One of the greatest mistakes people make when life gets hard is withdrawing into isolation. Do you not know that in those lonely spaces, sorrow and fear usually gain a stronger voice? But joy will often come alive when you share life with others who can encourage you in faith. Ecclesiastes 4:9–10 says, ***"Two are better than one... For if they fall, the one will lift up his fellow: but woe to him that is*** *alone when he falleth.* " This means that surrounding yourself with people who can speak life, who will remind you of God's promises, and who can encourage you to keep moving forward is a practical step that sustains joy. Even if your past was full of betrayal, do not let that stop you from finding godly companionship today.

- **Serve Others Even When You Are Hurting**

It may sound strange, but one of the quickest ways to experience joy is to look beyond yourself and serve others. Philippians 2:4 says, *"Look not every man on his own things, but every man also on the things of others."* When you step out of your pain long enough to bring comfort, help, or encouragement to someone else, you will realize that your own heart also becomes lighter. Joy usually grows when you stop obsessing over your own wounds and allow God to use you as a channel of healing for others. That does not mean you ignore your struggles, but it also means you must refuse to let them trap you in self-pity.

- **Feed Your Spirit Daily**

Another practical step is to constantly nourish your spirit with the Word of God, because joy cannot thrive in an empty or neglected heart. Jeremiah 15:16 says, *"Thy words were found, and I did eat them; and thy word was unto me the joy and rejoicing of mine heart."*

Every time you read and meditate on Scripture, you are feeding your spirit with joy-producing truth. You cannot expect to live joyfully while starving your soul. Set aside time each day, even if it is just a chapter or a few verses, and let God's Word sink into your heart.

- **Learn to Praise in the Dark**

One of the hardest but most powerful steps is to praise God even when your circumstances give you no reason to. Remember Paul and Silas in Acts 16, beaten and locked in prison, yet they prayed and sang praises to God, and suddenly the prison doors flew open. That is the power of praise. Psalm 34:1 says, *"I will bless the Lord at all times: his praise shall continually be in my mouth."* Notice the phrase "at all times", not only when everything is going right. Praise can shift your atmosphere, silence the enemy, and fill your heart with a great level of joy that cannot be explained.

- **Rest in God's Assurance of Victory**

Also, joy will become your daily companion when you rest in the truth that God has already given you victory. Deuteronomy 31:8 tells us, *"And the Lord, he it is that doth go before thee; he will be with thee, he will not fail thee, neither forsake thee: fear not, neither be dismayed."*

This means that no matter what you face, whether the painful memories of the past, the struggles of the present, or the uncertainties of the future, you can walk in joy because God has already gone ahead of you. You are not fighting for victory; you are living from victory, and that perspective alone can flood your heart with unshakable joy if you begin to meditate on it today.

In truth, every single day you have a choice, a choice to either surrender to despair or to step into the joy God has already promised. I mean it when I say that you do not have to wait for life to be perfect before you can live joyfully because joy is not dependent on circumstances but on Christ.

CHAPTER NINE

FAITH AS YOUR GATE TO JOY

Living Beyond the Prison of Your Past

There is a reason why so many people, even after years of attending church or hearing the Word of God, still find themselves trapped in cycles of pain, betrayal, disappointment, and hopelessness, and the reason is simple: they have not yet learned to live by faith. I was once there, and in those days of my pain, I never really knew what I was doing wrong. But what I am about to teach you will revolutionize your life completely!

If you do not start living in faith, you will always interpret life through the dark lenses of your negative past, and when you do that, you will always unconsciously keep expecting the same betrayals, the same abuse, the same rejection, and the same pain to reappear in your future. And take note, you will usually get what you are expecting! Proverbs 23:7 says, *"For as he thinketh in his heart, so is he."* If your heart is still chained to the memories of yesterday's chaos, then every situation you encounter will look like a continuation of your suffering, even when God is presenting something new. This is why faith is not just a religious word, it is your lifeline! Faith will help you step out of the prison of your past and into the promise of God.

But what is faith?

Faith is your ability to live based on God's Word, because through His Word, you will begin to see as He sees and act as He expects. Hebrews 11:1 defines it clearly by saying, *"Now faith is the substance of things hoped for, the evidence of things not seen."* Simply put, faith is choosing to believe that God's Word is more real than the scars of your yesterday, more powerful than the pain of your today, and more trustworthy than the fears of your tomorrow. Without faith, joy will always remain a stranger to you, but when faith is alive in your heart, joy flows like a river that no storm can dry up.

Take Caution on Your Tongue

If you keep saying words like "I am weak, I am broken, I am helpless, I am hopeless," then how can you ever expect to live a joyful life? You will never rise higher than the level of your confession! Jesus said in Mark 11:23, *"For verily I say unto you, That whosoever shall say unto this mountain, Be thou removed, and be thou cast into the sea; and shall not doubt in his heart, but shall believe that those things which he saith shall come to pass; he shall have whatsoever he saith."*

Notice the repetition of the word "saith." Your words carry weight. Your mouth is a steering wheel that determines the direction of your life, and if you constantly speak the language of defeat, then defeat is all you will ever experience and joy will always be far from you. And the moment joy is far from you, all that will be left is for you to keep living in regret based on your past.

Are you getting why you must begin to speak faith intentionally? Stop magnifying your pain with your words, stop rehearsing your failures in conversations, and stop allowing your tongue to prophesy doom over your tomorrow simply because you have had a rough past! Instead, take hold of God's promises and declare them with conviction!

Say: *"I can do all things through Christ which strengtheneth me"* (Philippians 4:13).

Say: *"The Lord is my light and my salvation; whom shall I fear?"* (Psalm 27:1).

Say: *"God is my refuge and strength, a very present help in trouble"* (Psalm 46:1).

Words are some of the most powerful things in the universe today, and you need to realize that the same God who created the world by speaking it into existence has given you that same creative ability in word form. *"For he spake, and it was done; he commanded, and it stood fast"* (Psalm 33:9). When you conceive the Word of God in your heart, form it with your tongue, and release it out of your mouth in faith, it becomes creative power that will work for you and not against you.

What are you speaking over your life daily? Is it faith or fear? Joy or sorrow? Hope or despair?

Faith Brings Peace, Strength, and Victory

The beautiful thing about faith is that it does not just change your words, it changes your entire perspective because it will help you to stop seeing yourself as a victim of yesterday's wounds and start seeing yourself as a victor through Christ. Romans 8:15 reminds us, *"For ye have not received the spirit of bondage again to fear; but ye have received the Spirit of adoption, whereby we cry, Abba, Father."*

If this sinks into your heart, you will never be bound by fear or haunted by the shadow of your past anymore because faith will bring you into the reality of being a beloved child of God! This faith we are talking about will give you peace, hope, strength, courage, and victory over the world! Perhaps I would have died long ago. I made almost every negative error possible, and as far as I was concerned, there was a time when suicide was not such a bad idea; nevertheless, here I am today, telling you about the wonder of God. Why? Because I believed in the Lord and He did not fail me. Well, I want you to know that if He did it for me, then He can do the same for you. No past is worth the sacrifice of your joy in the present.

If you can make this decision to walk by faith today, you will stop trembling at every new challenge because you know that God has already promised, *"There shall no evil befall thee, neither shall any plague come nigh thy dwelling. For he shall give his angels charge over thee, to keep thee in all thy ways"* (Psalm 91:10–11). When you walk by faith, you can boldly declare with the Psalmist and say, "In the day of my trouble I will call upon thee: for thou wilt answer me" (Psalm 86:7).

Faith can sustain you when your present feels like hell on earth because it will remind you that God is bigger than your problem and your suffering does not define your destiny. You better believe me on this, you need this to rise from betrayal, to recover from abuse, to dream again after failure, and to keep moving when your body and soul are screaming to quit! Without faith, you will always surrender to the weight of your circumstances and the regrets that come from your past. But with faith, you can stand strong and keep pressing forward until joy breaks forth again in your life.

Growing in Faith Daily

Many people think faith is something you either have or do not have, when in reality, faith is something that grows! Romans 10:17 puts it this way: *"So then faith cometh by hearing, and hearing by the word of God."* If you want to live in joy, you must feed your faith daily with the Word of God, because the more you hear His Word, the more your faith will rise, and the more your faith rises, the less power your past has over you. It is not enough to pray once in a while, and it is not enough to glance at the Bible occasionally. You must make it your daily pursuit to grow in faith by praying continually, reading the Word consistently, confessing His promises regularly, and surrounding yourself with believers who can speak faith instead of fear into your heart. Hebrews 10:24–25 tells us not to forsake assembling with others because we need each other to stir up faith and good works.

Do not settle for a weak faith that collapses at the first sign of trouble. Pursue a strong faith that endures storms, that rises above setbacks, and that can refuse to bow to fear! Remember 2 Corinthians 5:7: *"For we walk by faith, not by sight."* Walking by sight will always remind you of your past failures, but walking by faith will always remind you of God's promises.

I am sure you have now seen that this is not optional if you want to live in joy! If you choose to live without faith, you are choosing to live in the shadows of your past, chained by memories of pain and ruled by expectations of failure. But if you choose to live by faith, you are opening the gate to joy, to peace, to strength, and to a future that is not defined by where you have been but by what God has spoken. Ask yourself, will I keep expecting the same betrayals, the same chaos, the same heartbreak, or will I rise in faith and expect the goodness of God in my life? Will I keep rehearsing my past, or will I begin to declare my future in line with His promises?

Faith is your gate to joy, and until you walk through that gate, you will remain stuck outside in sorrow.

CHAPTER TEN

CONQUERING THE PITFALLS TO VICTORY AND FAITH OVER YOUR PAST

As much as many people want, they have not been able to truly walk through the gate of faith into a life of joy and victory, and the reason is not because God's promises are lacking, nor because His power is too small to break the chains of yesterday from their lives. It is most often because certain pitfalls are continually robbing them of their ability to step fully into the life of faith that God has already provided. If you do not deal with these pitfalls in your own life, you will keep circling the same wilderness, tied to your painful past, weighed down by memories of betrayal, and living with the expectation that tomorrow will be just as bitter as yesterday. So how do you conquer?

Let me show you some of the major pitfalls and how you can overcome each one, so that you will be able to stand in faith and truly live free from the shadows of your past.

Pitfall 1: Believing More in Your Past Than in God's Word

The first pitfall is when you allow the memory of your pain to carry more authority in your life than the promises of God. If every time you hear "God loves you," your mind instantly replies, "But if He really loved me, why did He let that happen?" then you are placing your past on a higher throne than the living Word of God. This is not faith; it is bondage to memory, and you will never be free that way.

God's Word is eternal, sharper than a two-edged sword, and it has the final authority over every season of your life. The mistake many make is to treat the Word of God like a gentle suggestion instead of the unshakable truth.

How to overcome it: You must deliberately reprogram your mind by constantly confessing and meditating on what God says until it outweighs the voice of your past. You should also begin to take Romans 10:17 seriously and allow it to shape your life every day. The more you soak yourself in Scripture, the louder God's Word will be in your heart, and the quieter the voices of yesterday will become.

Pitfall 2: Expecting Pain Instead of Expecting Promise

The second pitfall is when people subconsciously expect more pain in the future because of the pain they experienced in the past. When you have been betrayed, used, or abused, your natural mind begins to assume that tomorrow will repeat the same cycle, so you guard yourself with suspicion, live small, and never dare to trust or hope again.

But as we have already explained, what you expect is usually what you will see in your life. When you expect failure, you will begin to walk in line with failure. When you expect heartbreak, you will interpret every action as a step toward heartbreak. What you expect is what you will begin to experience because expectation is a silent prayer and proof of faith in that direction.

How to overcome it: You must begin to replace every negative expectation in your heart with hope anchored in God's faithfulness and His Word. Lamentations 3:22–23 says, *"It is of the Lord's mercies that we are not consumed, because his compassions fail not. They are new every morning: great is thy faithfulness."* Instead of expecting betrayal, expect God's mercy. Instead of expecting abuse, expect His protection. Make it a habit to wake up every morning declaring, "Today is filled with new mercies for me."

Pitfall 3: Trying to Live by Sight Instead of Faith

The third pitfall is trying to measure God's power by what your eyes can see. People often say, "I'll believe God when I see results," but that is not faith; that is doubt dressed in religious clothing. If you are waiting to see before you believe, then you are still chained to your past, and your sight is limited by what has already happened.

When you read Hebrews 11:1, remember that faith is not a denial of reality; it is you declaring that God's truth is greater than your visible circumstances, and when you can live this way, you will always be victorious.

How to overcome it: You must train your spirit to believe before you see. Say to yourself daily, "I do not live by sight. I live by faith." Start small if you must. Believe God for peace in your heart, for a fresh smile on your face, for strength to get through one more day, and as your faith grows, you will begin to see as God sees.

Pitfall 4: The Comfort of Familiar Pain

It may sound strange at first, but many people secretly cling to their pain because it has become the only reality they know. When you have lived for years rehearsing the wounds, disappointments, and betrayals of the past, they can start to feel like a twisted form of comfort in such a way that letting go can begin to feel terrifying because it means stepping into something unfamiliar, even if that unfamiliarity is healing, freedom, and peace. And because of that fear, you may unconsciously choose the comfort of familiar pain rather than the unknown of faith.

Think about the children of Israel when they came out of Egypt. Even after God parted the Red Sea, gave them manna, and showed them miracles, they still longed for Egypt, saying, ***"Would to God we had died by the hand of the LORD in the land of Egypt, when we sat by the flesh pots, and when we did eat bread to the full"*** (Exodus 16:3). Egypt represented bondage, but it was familiar, and freedom required faith, so they resisted it.

How to overcome it: The only way to break free from the trap of familiar pain is to deliberately choose the discomfort of healing over the false comfort of bondage. Healing requires courage, and courage is not the absence of fear; it is moving forward despite fear. You must daily confess before God, "Lord, I release my grip on what has wounded me, and I choose to embrace the unknown of Your freedom."

Take a practical step by creating new habits that symbolize release. For example, write down the memories or pains you have clung to on pieces of paper, and then burn or tear them as an act of surrender. Also, replace the space those pains occupied with worship, new friendships, or service to others. The more you fill your life with new patterns of faith, the less room there will be for the false comfort of old wounds.

Pitfall 5: Refusing to Forgive

The fifth pitfall is the refusal to forgive, which is one of the greatest killers of victory over your past. Unforgiveness keeps you tied to the moment of your pain, and every time you relive the offense, you give it new life. In such an environment, victory and faith to overcome will not survive. Joy, faith, and victory can never thrive in a heart full of bitterness. Jesus Himself said in Mark 11:25 that when you stand praying, forgive, so that your Father may forgive you. This means unforgiveness not only keeps you bitter and tied to the past, it also blocks your prayers.

Many cling to unforgiveness because they think forgiving means excusing the wrong or pretending it did not happen. But forgiveness is not denial; it is release, and it is you handing the offender over to God's justice so that you will no longer carry the burden.

How to overcome it: Pray daily for the strength to forgive. Speak forgiveness even before you feel it. Say, "Lord, I choose to release this person into Your hands." Over time, your emotions will align with your decision. Forgiveness clears the soil of your heart so that the seed of faith can grow.

Pitfall 6: Living in Self-Condemnation

The sixth pitfall is when you refuse to forgive yourself. It's possible to believe that God has forgiven you, yet deep down you may continue to punish yourself for the mistakes of the past. Self-condemnation will tell you, "You are unworthy, you don't deserve happiness, and you will always fail." Such voices are nothing but the devil's attempt to keep strangling you with the past. But Romans 8:1 says, *"There is therefore now no condemnation to them which are in Christ Jesus."* If God Himself does not condemn you, then who are you to condemn yourself? Yet many choose to wear the chains of guilt rather than receive the robe of righteousness.

How to overcome it: It's time for you to accept God's forgiveness as final and absolute. Write this down somewhere you can see it: "My past is forgiven, my present is redeemed, and my future is secure."

When self-condemnation rises, remind yourself that Jesus' blood paid in full, and nothing you do can add to or subtract from that payment.

Pitfall 7: The Cycle of Rehearsing the Past

Another reason many do not walk in faith is that they have developed the habit of rehearsing their past over and over again in their minds. The mind is powerful, and what you constantly meditate on becomes the environment you live in. Proverbs 23:7 says, *"For as he thinketh in his heart, so is he."* When you replay the betrayals, the abuse, the shame, and the regrets, you chain yourself to an endless cycle of reliving what should have been buried long ago.

Faith and victory over the past cannot operate when the past dominates your imagination. They require you to envision God's promises, but when your mental screen is filled with yesterday's pain, there is no room for the vision of tomorrow.

- Ask yourself this: What images do I constantly allow to replay in my mind?
- Are they scenes of pain, or are they visions of God's promises fulfilled?

Paul gave the secret in Philippians 3:13–14: *"Forgetting those things which are behind, and reaching forth unto those things which are before, I press toward the mark for the prize of the high calling of God in Christ Jesus."* Forgetting does not mean erasing the memory; it means refusing to allow it to dictate your present reality.

Faith says: Yes, that happened, but God is doing a new thing in me, and I choose to see that instead.

How to overcome it: To silence the endless reruns of yesterday, you must train your mind to switch channels. When the enemy brings up those old scenes, interrupt the pattern with intentional declaration. Say out loud: "I refuse to dwell on the past. I set my mind on what God has promised."

A very practical tool is Scripture substitution. Each time a memory arises, immediately quote a scripture that affirms your future. For example, when you recall betrayal, declare: *"Though my father and my mother forsake me, then the Lord will take me up"* (Psalm 27:10). Keep a list of such verses close at hand. With time, your mind will start to play the promises of God more than the pain of the past. Faith cannot coexist with the constant replay of yesterday; by substitution, you give faith the room to breathe.

Pitfall 8: The Illusion of Control

Many people are not walking in faith and victory over their past because they believe that holding on to their pain gives them some form of control. You will hear them say things like, "I'll never let anyone hurt me again," and then they build walls of suspicion, bitterness, and distrust around their hearts. In their minds, this feels like protection. But the truth is, those walls will keep God's healing from reaching you. Jeremiah 17:5 says, *"Cursed be the man that trusteth in man, and maketh flesh his arm, and whose heart departeth from the LORD."* When you try to manage your own healing without God, you will end up creating prisons of self-protection that trap you even deeper in the past.

Faith requires surrender, not control. It means saying, "Lord, I don't have to keep rehearsing my pain to protect myself, because You are my shield, my defender, and my rock."

How to overcome it: You cannot heal while trying to be your own savior. To break this illusion, you must intentionally practice daily surrender. Start every morning with a prayer that says: "Lord, I surrender this day, my heart, and my past to You. I will not try to shield myself with fear, but I will let You be my shield."

Then put this surrender into practice. Instead of building walls of suspicion, build boundaries of wisdom. There's a difference! Walls will keep everyone out, including God's love, while boundaries will allow you to live wisely without becoming hard-hearted. Trust is not about putting yourself back in harm's way; it is about refusing to live in fear and bitterness. As you surrender control, you will also be making space for God to fight battles you were never designed to fight on your own.

Pitfall 9: Shame That Silences

One of the most crippling barriers is shame, and we discussed this in earlier chapters. You see, guilt will say, "I did something wrong," then shame will say, "I am something wrong." When shame settles into the soul, it silences faith and any hope for victory or a better life. People who live under shame often believe deep down that they do not deserve God's joy, peace, or future, so they always end up sabotaging their own lives. But the truth is that Christ already bore your shame. Hebrews 12:2 tells us that Jesus *"endured the cross, despising the shame, and is set down at the right hand of the throne of God."* That means shame has no authority to disqualify you because Christ already carried it away. Let me ask you, do you believe the lie of shame more than you believe the promise of God? If your answer is yes, then no wonder faith and victory over the past feel like a struggle.

How to overcome it: Shame loses its power when exposed to the light of truth. To overcome it, you must intentionally replace the lies of shame with the identity of Christ. Start a practice of identity confessions today. Each morning, say:

- "I am the righteousness of God in Christ Jesus" (2 Corinthians 5:21).
- "I am beloved. I am accepted in the Beloved" (Ephesians 1:6).

You can also share your story with safe and faith-filled believers who will not condemn you but will remind you of who you are in Christ. Shame often thrives in silence but dies in the presence of truth spoken aloud.

Pitfall 10: Dependency on Human Approval

Many people cannot walk in faith and victory over their past because they are waiting for human approval to validate their healing. They want the abuser to apologize, the betrayer to admit guilt, or the family to acknowledge their pain before they move forward. While all those things may feel nice, none of them are necessary for you to step into faith. Romans 8:31 clearly says, *"If God be for us, who can be against us?"* If the Creator of heaven and earth has declared you forgiven, healed, and free, why wait for the validation of man? Victory over your past demands that you take God at His word, not at man's response. If you keep waiting for someone else to affirm your healing, you are effectively saying that their voice has more authority than God's Word. That is idolatry in disguise.

How to overcome it: Tie your identity to God's verdict, not man's applause. Whenever you find yourself craving someone's validation, pause and ask yourself, "If God has already approved me, why am I waiting for man's permission to move forward?" Train your spirit to celebrate God's approval. Write down the scriptures where God affirms you, such as *"Ye are complete in Him"* (Colossians 2:10) and *"If God be for us, who can be against us?"* (Romans 8:31). Keep them in a place you can see daily and let these words become louder than the silence or rejection of people.

Pitfall 11: Fear of Disappointment

For many people, the greatest barrier is fear, fear that if they dare to believe again, hope again, love again, or trust God's promise again, they will be disappointed. This fear is quiet but can be very powerful. It will tell you, "Don't expect too much, don't trust too deeply, and don't believe too boldly." Fear of disappointment is rooted in unbelief about God's character. Psalm 34:5 says, *"They looked unto him, and were lightened: and their faces were not ashamed."* In other words, nobody who has truly trusted God has ended up in disgrace.

How to overcome it: Over time, both through my life and the study of God's Word, I have realized that fear of disappointment is only broken when you step out in actions backed with prayer and wisdom from God's Spirit. Instead of waiting for perfect courage, start by trusting God in one specific area today. For example, pray for something small but meaningful, and write down the answer when it comes. Over time, these little testimonies build an unshakable confidence that God is trustworthy, and you will be able to overcome every fear of disappointment that keeps you from experiencing the life God has designed for you.

Also, replace "What if God fails me?" with "What if I miss what God has already prepared because I refuse to believe?"

Pitfall 12: Spiritual Laziness

Many are failing to walk in faith and victory because they are spiritually lazy. They want freedom from the past, but they do not want to stay in prayer, study the Word, or discipline their thoughts. They almost expect faith to be automatic, but faith is a muscle that must be exercised. If you are not filling your heart with God's Word daily, how will your faith ever grow? If you are not praying, how will you hear His voice? If you are not fellowshipping with believers, how will you be strengthened?

The reality is that your past will always shout louder if you refuse to feed your faith.

Here are some reflective questions to challenge yourself:

- How much time am I really investing in the Word of God each day?
- Do I spend more hours rehearsing my past than meditating on His promises?
- Am I lazy in prayer, or am I pressing into God for strength?

Faith and victory require effort, and if you are unwilling to put in the effort, you will remain trapped in the chains of yesterday instead of stepping into the victory of today.

How to Overcome It: I cannot say it enough: victory and faith are not automatic! They grow through intentional practice. Therefore, to overcome laziness, you must begin to build a disciplined routine of Word, prayer, and fellowship. Start small but be consistent. It could be fifteen minutes of prayer in the morning, one chapter of scripture daily, and weekly fellowship with believers. Do not despise these little disciplines, because they are what you need to build the muscles of faith so you can begin to thrive in life.

I will also like you to make it practical by setting reminders, joining a Bible plan, or finding an accountability partner. It may feel difficult at first, but consistency produces strength, and as you stay at it, it will soon become natural to you.

It's Time to Act!

Now that you know these pitfalls and how you can overcome them, the question is, will you keep falling into them, or will you rise above them? Victory is not theory; it must be experienced. If you truly want to stop living as a prisoner of your past, then you must deliberately tear down these obstacles. You must choose to accept and believe God's Word and His love over your memories, to expect His promises over your pain, to walk by faith and not by sight, to discipline your tongue, to forgive others, forgive yourself, and to walk daily in the discipline of faith.

Here are some questions I want you to meditate on before going to bed today:

- Do you believe your past is stronger than the blood of Jesus, or will you trust that His sacrifice is enough?
- Will you keep speaking words of defeat, or will you fill your mouth with life?
- Will you let bitterness harden your heart, or will you forgive so that faith can flow freely again?

- Will you keep waiting for faith to "just happen," or will you build it daily like a muscle?

The choice is yours, but mark my words: you can choose joy, you can choose peace, and you can choose freedom from the chains of your past.

CHAPTER ELEVEN

THINK ON THESE THINGS

What Do You Spend Your Mind On

Even as we slowly begin to approach the close of this book, I quickly need to point out that one of the most overlooked truths about human experience is that your life will never rise above the quality of your thoughts. Yes, no matter what has happened to you or what you are going through right now, your mind will always be the place where the battles of freedom or bondage are won or lost. For me, during those dark and painful days, I was not only weighed down by the cruelty of certain people or the mistakes I made, but by what I constantly fed my mind with. Looking back now, I realize that my thoughts were like a river flowing endlessly in the direction of pain, regret, and anger, and that current was continually dragging me deeper into despair every single day.

Paul, under the inspiration of the Spirit, gave us in Philippians 4:8 not just a casual encouragement but a divine prescription, a spiritual filter through which every thought must be tested. When applied faithfully, this Scripture can become a chain breaker that will set your inner life free from the captivity of your past.

Philippians 4:8 says, *"Finally, brethren, whatsoever things are true, whatsoever things are honest, whatsoever things are just, whatsoever things are pure, whatsoever things are lovely, whatsoever things are of good report; if there be any virtue, and if there be any praise, think on these things."* Now let us discuss each element individually, because each of them carries a depth of power that can transform the way you think and thereby how you live.

- **"Whatsoever things are TRUE"**

According to Paul in this verse, the starting point for your mind is truth, because lies are the devil's oldest weapon and he thrives by magnifying pain with deception. When you spend your thoughts on what is false, such as "I am worthless," "I can never rise again," or "my past defines me," you are unknowingly tying yourself to chains that Christ has already broken for you. The Bible says, *"And ye shall know the truth, and the truth shall make you free"* (John 8:32). Truth does not deny that your past was painful, but truth declares that the blood of Jesus has cleansed you, that God is still your Father, and that your story is not over.

Truly, spending your mind on truth will build for you a foundation where lies will lose their grip, and in that light, the shadows of your past will never be able to dominate you anymore.

- **"Whatsoever things are HONEST"**

How about honesty? Honesty here speaks of nobility, integrity, and things that carry dignity before God. The human mind can easily drift toward crooked imaginations, bitterness, and self-pity, but Paul says that you are to discipline your thoughts toward what is honorable.

When your mind meditates on what is honest, you will stop feeding the devil's accusations and instead begin to see yourself as God sees you: redeemed, valuable, and called to righteousness. Romans 6:18 says, *"Being then made free from sin, ye became the servants of righteousness."* This is honesty at the deepest level, acknowledging who you now are in Christ instead of constantly reliving who you were in sin or what others did to you in darkness.

- **"Whatsoever things are JUST"**

To think on what is just means to position your thoughts in line with God's justice and fairness. Many remain bound to the past because they replay unfairness, asking why life treated them so cruelly. But when your mind is consumed with that, you will obviously forget that God is the righteous Judge who will always do right.

Spending your thoughts on what is just is not just about not demanding revenge; it is also about trusting His justice and knowing He has the final word. This will free you from the endless cycle of bitterness, because your mind will no longer be fixated on how people wronged you but on the truth that God's throne is established in righteousness.

- **"Whatsoever things are PURE"**

So what does it mean to keep your mind on things that are pure? Purity in thought is a weapon against the contamination of past sins and memories. The enemy will always try to replay filthy experiences or shameful chapters of your life in your mind. But when you choose to meditate on what is pure, rather than continually thinking of your past failures and negative experiences, you will be washing your inner world in the cleansing waters of God's Word.

When purity dwells in your thought life, it flushes out the poison of guilt and the dirt of condemnation. Instead of replaying what was unclean in your past, your mind will become saturated with holy desires, godly images, and a renewed vision of yourself as cleansed and set apart.

- **"Whatsoever things are LOVELY"**

To think on what is lovely means to focus your mind on what is beautiful, gracious, and life-giving. Stop thinking of all the negativity of your past! During seasons of pain, your mind will naturally gravitate toward ugliness, harsh words spoken against you, betrayals, and even missed opportunities. Paul commands us to set our imagination on what reflects God's beauty. This is not fantasy; it is spiritual discipline.

Psalm 48:14 says, *"For this God is our God for ever and ever: he will be our guide even unto death."* His presence in your life is lovely, His faithfulness is beautiful, and His grace is full of sweetness. As you turn your thoughts toward these, the heavy atmosphere of your past will begin to lose its stranglehold, because loveliness has a healing power that darkness cannot contend with.

- **"Whatsoever things are of GOOD REPORT"**

Many are trapped in the prison of their past because they seem to always spend their thoughts on reports of failure, gossip, betrayal, and disaster, both from their own painful experiences and from the experiences of others.

But from today, I want you to know that when you feed your mind on negative reports, it creates a cycle of fear and despair that not only chains you to the past but also begins to pollute your present. This is why the Bible says you must dwell on what is of good report! A good report is what God has said about you, things like *"I can do all things through Christ which strengtheneth me"* (Philippians 4:13*), "The Lord is the strength of my life"* (Nehemiah 8:10), and *"I let the peace of God rule in my heart"* (Colossians 3:15).

When these reports dominate your inner dialogue, the bad reports of your past will lose their power, because your spirit is now strengthened by the testimony of God's promises rather than the echo of your pain.

- **"If there be any VIRTUE"**

Virtue speaks of moral excellence, courage, and strength of character. The reality is that the past often cripples people by making them feel weak, stained, or unworthy, and if you keep your mind on such things, you can forget about being able to go beyond your past. But today, accept what God is saying. He is calling you to feed your mind with thoughts of virtue. This means thinking about who you are becoming through Christ, meditating on the fruit of holiness that now grows in your life, and recognizing the grace that has empowered you to stand.

Romans 6:22 says, *"But now being made free from sin, and become servants to God, ye have your fruit unto holiness, and the end everlasting life."* To think on virtue is to celebrate the transformation that has begun in you. It may be slow; nevertheless, you can be sure that it will surely break the chains of shame and regret that may have clouded your life because of your past.

- **"If there be any PRAISE"**

Finally, Paul directs us to dwell on things that are worthy of praise. This is very important because praise is a perspective shifter. When you train your thoughts to magnify God's goodness rather than your past failures, you will be able to turn your inner gaze upward. Praise will then be able to reorient your heart to gratitude, and gratitude will dismantle the strongholds of despair.

Jesus Himself said in Matthew 6, *"Take no thought for your life, what ye shall eat, or what ye shall drink; nor yet for your body, what ye shall put on… your heavenly Father knoweth that ye have need of all these things."* This is the essence of praise in your thoughts. You must refuse to rehearse worry and choose instead to exalt the God who provides.

Looking at all these, notice how Philippians 4:8 covers every possible arena of the human mind:

- Truth over lies
- Honesty over corruption
- Justice over bitterness
- Purity over filth
- Loveliness over ugliness
- Good report over bad report
- Virtue over weakness
- Praise over despair

Each is like a pillar holding up a fortress for your mind, and when your inner world is built upon these, I assure you that the ruins of your past will never be able to overrun you again.

You must train yourself to **"THINK ON THESE THINGS!"** It is not a suggestion; it is an imperative because your thought life will either enslave you to your history or usher you into the liberty of your destiny. What you spend your mind on determines whether your past continues to torment you or whether God's Word will reshape you into a new creation walking in victory.

PRACTICAL STEPS TO KEEP YOUR MIND ON THE RIGHT THINGS

Practice the Art of Catching Your Thoughts Early

The first key to keeping your mind in the right direction is to train yourself to become aware of what you are thinking about in the first place. The problem many face is that they often allow their thoughts to run freely without any supervision, and before they realize it, their mind has already wandered into regret, bitterness, or fear.

A simple exercise you can do is to pause several times a day and ask yourself, "What am I thinking about right now? Where is my mind dwelling?" If you catch yourself replaying old hurts or imagining negative outcomes, stop right there and say out loud, "No, I refuse to think this way." Then replace it with a Scripture, a truth about God's promises, or even a simple declaration like, "God loves me, and my future is bright."

Think of your thoughts like a train. You cannot stop a train from passing, but you can choose not to climb on board. The moment you notice a "negative train" pulling in, don't get on it. Let it pass, and deliberately board a train filled with truth and hope.

Use the Power of Scripture to Redirect Your Mind

The reality is, you cannot overcome wrong thoughts simply by telling yourself, "I won't think about this anymore." Your mind cannot remain empty; it must be filled with something stronger, and that is where the Word of God comes in. Colossians 3:16 says that you should allow the word of Christ to dwell in you richly. When Scripture dwells richly in you, it becomes the material your mind will automatically draw upon when it starts to wander.

Today, I want you to write down a list of five Scriptures that directly speak to your struggles: maybe one about peace (Philippians 4:7), one about strength (Philippians 4:13), one about God's care (Matthew 6:26), one about forgiveness (Romans 8:1), and one about hope (Jeremiah 29:11). Then, carry this list with you or keep it in your phone. Whenever you notice your mind slipping into negative patterns, immediately speak one of those Scriptures aloud and think about it slowly. Picture it, repeat it, and let it soak in until your mind is no longer stuck on the wrong track.

This will work like a reset button. Instead of just trying to "stop" a wrong thought, you will be actively replacing it with a higher truth, which is far more effective.

Create Mental Triggers That Shift Your Focus

Another powerful practice is to set up "mental triggers." These are simple actions or reminders that can immediately pull your thoughts back into alignment when they drift. For example, you can decide that every time you catch yourself worrying, you will immediately whisper, "Lord, I trust You," or even sing a short line of a hymn like "Great is Thy Faithfulness." These small acts serve as anchors that remind your mind to reset.

Practically, choose one trigger for one specific area of struggle. If you often dwell on regret, decide that the moment you notice those memories rising, you will place your hand over your heart and say, "I am forgiven, I belong to God, and I move forward." If you often worry about the future, decide that you will look upward and say, "God has already gone ahead of me." Over time, your brain begins to associate those old thought patterns with your new trigger, and slowly, they lose their power over you.

It's like training a muscle. The more consistently you respond with your trigger, the stronger your mental discipline becomes.

Feed Your Mind Daily with the Right Inputs

You cannot expect your mind to think right if you are constantly feeding it with the wrong materials. The truth is, your mind will always reflect what you expose it to most frequently, just like a sponge will always release what it has absorbed. If you are filling your day with conversations, movies, music, or social media that are negative, dirty, or hopeless, then you will struggle to keep your thoughts on what is pure, lovely, and of good report.

A very practical step is to make sure you are giving your mind daily foods that are in line with Philippians 4:8. Start your day with a Psalm or a worship song that lifts your spirit, replace gossip-filled conversations with uplifting ones, and choose books, podcasts, and messages that will build your faith instead of tearing it down.

A mental exercise you can try is that at the end of each day, ask yourself, "What did I feed my mind with today? Did it help me think on what is true, pure, and lovely?" If you notice you have been feeding on the wrong things, don't condemn yourself; simply adjust for the next day, and over time, this habit will completely change the atmosphere of your inner life.

Practice the Discipline of Gratitude and Praise

This is a very powerful step, so do not ignore or trivialize it in any way. You must train your mind to focus on gratitude and praise instead of complaints, worrying, or anxieties. Negative thoughts usually thrive in an atmosphere of complaining, but they will die in an atmosphere of thanksgiving and praise. Psalm 34:1 says, *"I will bless the Lord at all times: his praise shall continually be in my mouth."* Take note of the phrase "at all times", not only when things are easy, but also when life feels painful or uncertain!

A simple daily exercise is to write down three things you are grateful for every morning, no matter how small. It could be your health, a friend, food on your table, or even the fact that God woke you up today. Then, as you go through the day, whenever a negative thought arises, consciously replace it with one of those points of gratitude. For example, if your mind starts replaying a painful past event, stop and say, "Lord, I thank You that even though that happened, You kept me alive, and You are still guiding me today."

Another practice is to set aside two minutes, three times a day, just to praise God aloud. You don't need music, and you don't even need a long amount of time; just simply say, "Lord, You are good, and I praise You for Your love." These short bursts of praise are like oxygen for your mind, constantly refreshing your inner atmosphere and keeping it fresh for a joyful and hopeful life.

At the end of the day, keeping your mind stayed on the right things is not about wishing or hoping; it is about practicing daily disciplines that will help you retrain the way you think. By catching your thoughts early and redirecting them, you will be able to build a fortress in your thought life that the past cannot easily break into. This is how you will be able to begin living out Philippians 4:8 in practice, not as a distant ideal, but as a daily experience!

Believe me, if you begin to apply these steps consistently, you will soon discover that your mind no longer runs freely into old pasts of pain but becomes a garden where peace, joy, and hope are constantly growing. And that, my friend, is the pathway to breaking free from the chains of yesterday and living fully in the joy God has designed for you because you chose to accept Him, His love, and His principles.

God bless you.

CONCLUSION

Life has a way of leaving marks on our souls, and if you are honest with yourself, you will admit that those marks sometimes feel more like wounds that never heal. Perhaps you have carried shame for years, perhaps you have hidden pain so deeply that even your closest friends do not know how much you cry when you are alone, or maybe you walk around smiling while secretly feeling like you are slowly dying on the inside. As you know, I have been there, and I can say that I completely understand how you feel. Every person has a story, and many of those stories are filled with regret, disappointment, rejection, and mistakes that cannot be erased. But here is what I need you to understand right now: "Your past was never meant to be the end of your story."

You may have lived with chains so long that you started to believe they were part of you, but I assure you they are not. The anger, the bitterness, the guilt, the loneliness, the rejection, none of these were meant to define your future. You may think that because of what you have done, or what was done to you, your life will never be whole again, but I want you to hear me clearly: "God never designed your life to be a constant rehearsal of pain." He wants to step in, He wants to break the chains, and He wants to show you what it means to live free.

Romans 5:8 tells us that God showered His love toward us even when we were yet sinners. He did not wait for you to become perfect, and He did not demand that you clean yourself up before He would love you. No! He loved you right there in the middle of the mess, right there in the brokenness, right there when you thought you were worthless and may have given up on yourself. But He will never give up on you.

So the question you must now answer is: how much longer will you let the chains of the past hold you down? How long will you keep silent when your heart is screaming for help? You must decide today, and that time is now. Do not wait for tomorrow, because tomorrow is never promised. Do not tell yourself that you will surrender later, because later may never come. The time to rise is now, and the time to accept the help of God is today.

Maybe you feel like no one understands what you are going through, and in a human sense, you might be right, but Jesus understands more than you think. He knows every detail of your story. He has seen every tear you cried, He has felt every weight you carried, and He has never once turned His face away from you. I know it is not easy to trust when you have been hurt. I know it feels risky to open your heart after so much disappointment. But what I can guarantee is that you will never regret giving everything to God and accepting Him as your ever-present help. The only regret you will ever have is if you keep waiting, if you keep holding back, and if you keep letting fear tell you that you are not worthy.

You do not have to stay broken, you do not have to live in chains, and you do not have to be defined by your past. God's love is greater than every failure, every sin, every scar, and every wound. He wants to rewrite your story. He wants to heal your heart. He wants to give you joy where there was sorrow, peace where there was torment, and hope where there was despair.

So rise up today and take courage, open your mouth, and begin to talk to Him. Tell Him your pain, tell Him your fear, tell Him your past, and tell Him your secrets. He will not turn you away. He is waiting for you, not tomorrow, not next week, but right now. This is your moment, this is your call, and this is your invitation to freedom. Do not waste it.

The chains are already broken, the prison door is already open, and the way forward has already been made. All that remains is for you to step out and walk into the life that God has been waiting to give you all along.

www.ingramcontent.com/pod-product-compliance
Lightning Source LLC
Chambersburg PA
CBHW051216120626
46547CB00013B/1372